IRISH CATHOLIC SPIRITUALITY

To
Sr Margaret King, R.S.M.
Galway
cara dhil agus anam-chara
dom féinig agus do mhórán.
Go mba fada buan í.

John J. Ó Ríordáin, C.SS.R.

Irish Catholic Spirituality

Celtic and Roman

the columba press

First published in 1998 by
the columba press
55A Spruce Avenue, Stillorgan Industrial Park, Blackrock, Co Dublin

Cover by Bill Bolger
Origination by The Columba Press
Printed in Ireland by Colour Books Ltd, Dublin

Reprinted 2004

ISBN 1 85607 243 6

Acknowledgements
The author and publisher gratefully acknowledge the permission of the following to use material which is in their copyright: The Editor of *The Furrow*; Brendan Kennelly for *The Tree of Life*; Constable Publishers for *Selections from Ancient Irish Poetry* by Kuno Meyer; Irish Academic Press for *The Correspondence of Daniel O'Connell* by M. R. O'Connell; Gill and Macmillan for *The Hidden Ireland* by Daniel Corkery, *The Life and Writings of St Patrick* by J. Healy, *Old Ireland* by R. McNally, *Old Irish Links with France* by R. McNally, *It All Happened* by S. Fenton, and *The Irish Catholic Experience* by Patrick Corish; Veritas Publications for *Patrick in his own words* by Joseph Duffy; The Royal Irish Academy for quotations from *Ériu*; Messenger Publications for *Our Mass, Our Life* by Diarmuid Ó Laoghaire; University of Chicago Press for *Early Irish Literature* by Myles Dillon; Oxford University Press for *Early Irish Lyrics* edited and translated by Gerard Murphy; Burns & Oates for *Early Irish Laws and Institutions* by E. MacNeill. We have also applied for the following permissions: CTS London for *Adict for Christ* by F. Johnston; Geoffrey Chapman for *The Changing Face of Ireland* by Desmond Fennell; An Sagart for *Sages, Saints and Storytellers* by D. Ó Corráin; The Educational Company of Ireland for *Irish Life in the Seventeenth Century* by E. McLysaght and *Dánta Dé* edited by L. McKenna; The Mercier Press for *The Farm by Lough Gur* by Mary Carberry and *Irish Classical Poetry* by Eleanor Knott; Secker and Warburg for *Background Music* by Christy Brown; The Longman Group for *Annals of Loch Cé* edited by W. M. Hennessy; The Devin Adair Company for *The Story of the Irish Race* by Seamus MacManus; W. Heffer & Son for *The Early Monastic Schools* by W. G. Hanson.
We have made every effort to contact copyright holders and seek their permission to use their material. If any involuntary infringement of copyright has occurred, we offer our apologies and will correct any error in future editions.

Contents

Abbreviations

AHR	American Historical Review
CIH	The Course of Irish History
HIC	A History of Irish Catholicism
IER	Irish Ecclesiastical Record
ITQ	Irish Theological Quarterly
ITS	Irish Text Society
KAJ	Kerry Archaeological Journal

Foreword

When I wrote *Irish Catholics* more than twenty years ago it was welcomed by many as a good introduction to Celtic spirituality. Since then there has been an explosion of publications on matters Celtic and I have been persuaded to re-issue this volume, long out of print, in revised and updated form and under a slightly altered title.

It is with heartfelt gratitude that I acknowledge the contribution of Fr Richard Tobin, CSSR, for his generosity in proof-reading and for his many insightful suggestions, virtually all of which I have been happy to incorporate. For access to library material I acknowledge a debt of gratitude to the Dominican Friars and to the staff of the County Library in Dundalk, especially Ms Kathy Murphy; to the staff of the National Library of Ireland, Dublin and that of Mary Immaculate College, Limerick. It is also a pleasure for me to acknowledge my deep satisfaction at the unfailing courtesy and efficiency of Mr Seán O Boyle and the staff of Columba Press.

John J. O Ríordáin, CSSR
Feast of Cellach of Armagh, 1998

Introduction

The Catholic Church in Ireland is living through difficult times.
We are at once trying to cope with swift and far-reaching social
and political change together with the evolution of our Catholic
faith in the light of the Second Vatican Council. In the inevitable
confusions and uncertainties of such a time, many people wonder and ask what is the cause of the turmoil. In less sensitive mo-
ments I attempt to answer that question; in more attentive mood
I simply listen and wonder too.

There would have to be many strands to an adequate answer.
In this book I try to weave just a few of those strands. In this time
of transition, there is, inevitably, a generation that knew another
kind of Ireland, another kind of Catholic Church, while growing
up around them is a generation that did not. Both generations
need to reflect on Liam De Paor's observation that , 'No matter
how pluralistic Ireland may be or may become, and how much
religious belief may wane or change in the future, the historical
fact of fifteen centuries of Christianity remains. It is one of the
most important facts of Irish history. The obvious should not be
overlooked. Christianity in a thousand ways has shaped the history of Ireland.'[1]

The Irish spiritual story involves the underlying pagan
strand into which the Christian gospel was originally grafted.
As lived throughout the Christian centuries, it has come under
the influence of Viking, Norman and English culture and values.
It has been tested by persecution and overlain with the post-
Tridentine theology of the Counter-Reformation. In more recent
times (since the nineteenth century) it has been married – un-
happily, some would claim – to an imported italianate piety that
was never fully assimilated.

A particular factor that has contributed to the change of Catholic attitudes and practice over recent decades is the upsetting of that delicate balance between the church as institution and the church as community of faith in Christ Jesus. (In using the word church here I am referring to the Catholic Church in Ireland; but the maintaining of the balance between institution and faith community is not merely a Catholic or an Irish concern).

In a tentative analysis of what he called 'atheism Irish style,' Michael Paul Gallagher, SJ, noted that the atheism peculiar to Ireland is not based on philosophical grounds but on 'a disenchantment with the externals of church life and practice,' an alienation. 'By alienation I mean feelings of withdrawal, even of revulsion from something in which one is externally involved. Obviously alienation from externals can lead to the death of the internals, in so far as those internals of faith in Christ were truly alive or mature in the first place.' Fr Gallagher adds:

> Another comparatively recent phenomenon may be called the religious unbeliever, someone who leaves the church to pursue new cults often of Eastern origin or who attaches himself to fundamentalist Christian groups; the key factor here lies in an appeal to spiritual aspirations beside which the church practice of his upbringing seemed dead and superficial. Once again, one comes back to an alienation from a seemingly externalist religion as a trait linking several forms of unbelief.[2]

A form of atheism to which Michael Paul Gallagher did not directly refer surfaced later in a television discussion between two politicians. The one was a practising Catholic, the other claimed to be an atheist. At one point the Catholic said to his friend: 'You're not an atheist, Paddy; you're just a big lazy lump that won't get up and go to Mass on Sunday!' For historical reasons, to be explored later, 'going to Mass', like not eating meat on a Friday in former times, has become the touchstone of Irish Catholic practice; though in point of fact there may be little prayerfulness or living faith in the lives of some of the Mass-

goers, and the manner of eucharistic celebration may be anything but inspiring. The *Mystery*, so essential to all spirituality
and so dear to Celtic Ireland, may often be dimmed or extin-
guished.

Because of the strength and depth and tradition of Catholic
faith in the average Irish person, their abandoning of the Mass or
other expressions of their Catholic faith and culture does not
come easily. In this regard, Fr Geoffrey O'Connell, one of my
Redemptorist confreres, once remarked that, when an
Englishman leaves the Catholic Church he does so quietly; but if
an Irishman decides to do the same he has to sweep all the delph
off the dresser as he goes out the door; and then he cannot refrain from continuing to lob stones onto the roof just to make
sure he is not forgotten.

My own experience of Irish Catholics who are alienated from
their church is that they seem to reject the whole church because
of a practical aspect of its institutional face which happens to be
uncongenial to them; whereas a lot of the essential elements in
the church still appeal to them:

> Yet sometimes when the sun comes through a gap
> These men know God the Father in a tree:
> The Holy Spirit is the rising sap,
> and Christ will be the green leaves that will come
> At Easter from the sealed and guarded tomb.[3]

In the chapters of this book I strive to highlight, within an historical context, a number of the constant elements of Irish Catholic
spirituality. Whether they are plainly visible or only occasionally
break the surface, they are recurring traits with which Irish
Catholics of any century might identify. These constant elements are significant, very significant if we subscribe to the view
of the French anthropologist Marret that 'survivals are no mere
wreckage of the past, but are likewise symptomatic of those tendencies of our common nature which have the best chance of
surviving in the long run.'[4] These 'survivals,' as I have isolated
them, include:

1. Little or no distinction between the material and spiritual world and an equal feeling of at-homeness with this world and the other world.

2. A spirituality in harmony with nature, accepting it, respecting it, in love with it, even in its more violent expressions.

3. A natural religious spirit in the people – 'among your earthiest words the angels stray,'[5] as Patrick Kavanagh said of his mother.

4. Giving a low priority to organisational matters – 'plans are only for people of limited vision,' a North Cork Hedge Schoolmaster stoutly maintained.[6]

5. A traditional faith firmly rooted in the sacred scriptures which the people both knew and loved.

6. A great love for and devotion to the person of Christ, especially in his passion and the Mass.

7. A corresponding love for Mary, the angels and the saints, – above all for Mary as Mother of God.

8. The quality of *muintearas* – the community, communion, friendship, relationship, kindness, alliance with the Lord and his household in this present life and in the other world.

9. The combining of a strong notion of 'localness' with a deep sense of communion with the Body of Christ at a universal level; and an all-embracing congregational quality in both liturgical and popular prayer.

10. Hospitality as a living expression of the gospel – the guest is none other than the living Christ.

11. Penance and self-denial as a means of entering into the death of Christ.

12. The pilgrimage phenomenon.

13. A close bond of unity with the dead, giving a sense of fidelity to and continuity with the past.

14. A sense of humour which saves most of us from following extremes.

Against this background, Vatican II's message of freedom and
fidelity is music to the ears; for our popular religious tradition is
at once faithful to the point of apparent fatalism and fresh, free-
flowing, and unpredictable as a mountain stream.

> A fragrant prayer upon the air
> My child taught me,
> Awaken there, the morn is fair,
> The birds sing free.
> Now dawns the day, awake and pray
> And bend the knee,
> The lamb who lay beneath the clay
> Was slain for thee.[7]

CHAPTER 1

The 'Celtic Church'

That St Patrick, Apostle of Ireland, was a tremendous missionary, one of the greatest of all time, is a fact that no knowledgeable person will deny. And it is an interesting thing that, in so far as we can judge, his mission methods in the fifth century and those advocated by the Congregation for the Propagation fo the Faith in relation to China in the seventeenth century and by Pope Paul VI in the twentieth, bear a remarkable similarity.[1] What each says in effect is this: take the people as you find them; build on what you have; disturb and change only where you must; listen to the people for they have wisdom aplenty; graft in the message of Christ without destroying the stock, because the people need roots.

Patrick's first introduction to Ireland was abrupt and without formality. Captured by an Irish raiding party on one of their sallies into Roman Britain, Patrick was enslaved in Ireland for six years in his late teens and early twenties. The years of captivity were not without profound benefit. The youth learned the language and ways of his captors. More importantly, he found himself as a man and interiorised his Christian faith.

But what of the island and its people? The island of Ireland lies in the North Atlantic on the fringe of Europe's continental shelf. Covering an area of about 32,000 square miles (or one third the size of the State of Oregon), it has been continually inhabited for some ten thousand years because the climate was mild and food was readily available from the fish in the rivers and the hunt on the hill. Among the successive waves of settlers that came to our shores, the most notable of all were the Celts.

Their coming, mostly in the latter half of the first millennium before Christ, ushered in the early Iron Age.

With the Celts came much of the myth and mystery, enchantment and romance, so often associated with the Irish and charmingly captured by Thomas Darcy McGee in his poem *The Celts*:

Long, long ago, beyond the misty space
Of twice a thousand years;
In Erin old there dwelt a mighty race
Taller than Roman spears;

Like oaks and towers they had a giant grace,
Were fleet as deers,
With wind and waves they made their 'biding place,
These western shepherd seers.

Great were their deeds, their passions and their sports;
With clay and stone
They piled on strath and shore those mystic forts,
Not yet o'erthrown.[2]

Commenting on what we might call the 'Celtic Image', Proinsias Mac Cana writes:

Down the ages there is a remarkable consistency in the comments of foreign observers writing about the Celts. Thus, while the popular notion of them as reflected in modern literature has undoubtedly been coloured by eighteenth and nineteenth century romanticism with its susceptibility to mist, magic and melancholy, it certainly did not originate there. In fact, many of the attributes which it ascribes to the Celts – eloquence, lyric genius, volatile temperament, prodigality, reckless bravery, ebullience, contentiousness, and so on – have a much longer lineage, appearing in the accounts by classical authors of two thousand years ago.[3]

By the time of Patrick's coming, Ireland had become a thoroughly Celtic land with a rich culture, satisfactory political and legal systems, and a body of religious beliefs and practices presided

over by its druids, and with an elaborate and fascinating mythology. The Roman Empire had expanded as far as neighbouring
Britain but fortunately for Ireland and for all of Europe, the im-
perial ambitions of Agricola were not realised and Ireland suffered no major intrusion until the advent of the Vikings in the
ninth century and the Anglo-Normans in the twelfth.

Consequently, the Irish social order, and the learned system
which it maintained, remained immune from violent assault
until long after Ireland had become Christian and Irish a written
language. This must be accounted one of the causes of the re-
markably conservative character of Irish learned tradition.[4] It
also accounts for Ireland being the sole representative in literature of the people of that great world beyond the borders of
Greece and Rome, whose thoughts have perished with their
lives.[5] Hence, as Kuno Meyer says, Ireland is 'the earliest voice
from the dawn of West-European civilisation.'[6] A vernacular literature only began to emerge in Britain and the Continent late
and slowly. It was not, for example, until 'the end of the
eleventh century that we find the beginnings of a national literature in France and Germany.'[7]

While paganism put up a stiff fight before its final over-
throw, Ireland was alone among all the countries of western
Europe whose conversion produced no martyrs. The process of
conversion was gradual and involved several missionaries
whose work spread over a considerable period of time. 'St
Patrick therefore,' writes Liam de Paor, 'doesn't occupy quite as
central a position in... the conversion of Ireland as some readers
might expect. Yet he deserves his pre-eminence because, as his
own writings make abundantly clear, he is of great interest in
himself.'[8]

Nevertheless the missionary work of Patrick was spectacu-
lar. As well as fulfiling his role as a fifth century bishop – look-
ing after an existing Christian community – he went the extra
mile, taking it upon himself to go into the heart of pagan territory
at the risk of life and limb, in order to win people for Christ at
the very end of the known world. In his own words, the apostle
tells us that he,

baptised thousands... ordained clerics everywhere... gave presents to kings... was put in irons... lived in daily expectation of murder, treachery or captivity... journeyed everywhere in many dangers, even to the farthest regions beyond which there lives nobody, [and rejoiced to see] the flock of the Lord in Ireland growing splendidly with the greatest care and the sons and daughters of kings becoming monks and virgins of Christ.[9]

But Patrick was fortunate in many respects. The people among whom he laboured were religious by nature. Ernest Renan says that the Celts were endowed with 'profound feeling and adorable delicacy'[10] in their religious instincts. And the Scottish collector, Alexander Carmichael, says: 'The people were sympathetic and synthetic, unable to see and careless to know where the secular began and the religious ended – an admirable union of elements in life for those who have lived it so truly and intensely as the Celtic races everywhere have done.'[11]

Among these warm-hearted people Patrick lived and moved for perhaps thirty years. He was sensitive to the people and their culture, using his diplomatic skills, approaching the right people in the right way, and observing due protocol in relation to the power-structure of the day. Contrary to popular opinion, Patrick was no simple-minded, inarticulate, incoherent missionary but a well-informed and faith-filled man, who saw himself as God's instrument in the conversion of Ireland. Far from disturbing traditional patterns of religious practice, he seems to have Christened them, adding new dimensions of vision and hope. From available sources, including his own *Confession of Grace* and his *Letter Excommunicating Coroticus*, it would seem that he missionised whole sections of totally pagan territory and established chains of local Christian communities, out of which a vigorous countrywide church would shortly emerge. Folk tradition has it that he cursed and that he blessed, but his writings show him to be overwhelmingly a man of blessings.[12]

Despite our modern wish to know more biographical facts

about Patrick, we should be grateful for what we do know: it is impressive – for a man of his time. Liam de Paor says that 'we know that he existed (and roughly when); that he was a bishop in Ireland; that he came from Britain where his father had been of the Roman official class and well-to-do; that he baptised large numbers of Irish people and devoted much of his life to this evangelising work. We know that his belief was (in the fifth century sense) Catholic, or orthodox, and not, for example, Arian.'[13] To this we can add Daniel Conneely's assessment that 'Although his *Confession of Grace* and *Letter Excommunicating Coroticus* are brief, [about twenty pages of a modern book] through them we know the kind of person he was and, although they were were written with specific purposes, they are so clearly and fully reasoned that they provide a cross-section of his whole theological understanding. They are astonishingly valuable indeed as a scripture of both his faith-life (i.e. his *life* with Christ, unseen but present, and, in and through Christ, with God the Father and the Spirit) and his belief-faith (i.e. what he assented to as revealed truth).'[14] As well as presenting the Catholic faith as 'life with Christ,' he also proclaimed 'the absolute value to Christ of every single human being everywhere,' and 'while being supremely active and practical, St Patrick always kept in sight, like an horizon, that his pastoral objective was transforming minds and hearts'[15] – making them like Christ. His scriptural quotations and allusions have led people to describe him as a man of one book. A closer reading of his writings reveals that he not only quotes or alludes to fifty-four of the seventy-three books of the bible, but also to at least twenty of the Church Fathers and eight Church Councils.[16]

Patrick had more than technical knowledge of the scriptures and the body of church tradition. He had internalised the Christian message to an extraordinary degree. His was a truly *living* faith. He had a profound appreciation of the in-dwelling Trinity in his heart and an equally strong experience of an all-enveloping love which we speak of as the Providence of God. In his *Confession* he writes:

When I had come to Ireland I tended herds every day and I
used to pray many times during the day. More and more my
love of God and reverence for him began to increase. My
faith grew strong and my zeal so intense that in the course of
a single day I would say as many as a hundred prayers, and
almost as many in the night. This I did even when I was in
the woods and on the mountains. Even in times of snow or
frost or rain I would rise before dawn to pray. I never felt the
worse for it; nor was I in any way lazy because, as I now realise, I was full of enthusiasm.[17]

Together with the daily crosses and frustrations of a missioner's
life, Patrick carried with him all his days scars of loneliness and
feelings of being alienated, plus a deep emotional hurt – a snub,
a rejection, a serious breach of confidence or a betrayal by somebody whom he considered to be a close friend. His singlemind-
edness is inspiring and his unwillingness to allow anyone to
mother him or compromise him is touchingly human and mildly
amusing:

Although I am unskilled in every way I have tried somehow
to avoid being spoiled by my Christian brothers, and by the
nuns and the devout women who used to offer me little presents unasked and would even leave some of their jewellery
on the altar. When I insisted on giving them back they were
offended. But mine was the long-term view and for that reason I used to take every precaution so that the heathens
might not catch me out on any issue concerning myself or the
work of my ministry.[18]

The question has been asked but not definitively answered: *was
St Patrick a monk?* There is, says Michael Herren, 'a tendency to
deny (or ignore the evidence) that Patrick experienced a monastic background or that he had a role to play in developing the
monastic character of the early mediaeval Irish church.'[19] He
goes on to say that,

it must be stated at the outset that we have no clear evidence that Patrick was a monk; we do not know precisely where, or even when, he came into contact with a monastic environment. Nor do we have direct and unambiguous evidence regarding the ecclesiastical organisation created by Patrick in Ireland, except, of course that he ordained clerics to baptise. Yet Patrick's writings provide much clear evidence about his attitudes towards monastic life (broadly defined) and regarding his role in developing that life in Ireland. The following assertions can be textually supported: (i) Patrick had a deep sympathy for a higher kind of religious life in which celibacy was the principal component. (ii) Patrick actively promoted this life among his Irish converts, both male and female. (iii) The creation and maintenance of 'virgins of Christ' was the goal closest to Patrick's heart.[20]

By the fifth century, monasticism in Western Europe was fairly well organised, but in Ireland we cannot point to any specific site and say with certainty that it is as early as that. More than likely Patrick's 'monks and virgins,' like their earlier counterparts in Palestine and Syria, lived in the family home or compound, in a room or building apart.[21]

The tendency towards monastic life in Irish Celtic Christianity accelerated to such a degree that, within a century of his death, new monasteries had superseded many of the old Patrician foundations as centres of religion and learning. Ultimately Ireland became unique in western Christendom in having its most important churches ruled by a monastic hierarchy, many of whom were not bishops.[22] In fact a monastic system replaced any previous administrative structure.

This extraordinary flowering of monasticism owes its origins to a number of factors, not least among them being: (a) the tendency in the Irish temperament towards an ascetic way of life; (b) the strong attractive personalities of the great monastic founders; (c) the influence of St Ninian's monastery (*Candida Casa*) in Scotland; (d) the emphasis placed on study in monastic life – particularly the study of the sacred scriptures – on which the Welsh reforming saints, Cadoc and Gildas, placed so much stress.[23]

Religious communities of women were less numerous but no less esteemed. The great monastery of St Brigid in Kildare was a double monastery for both men and women, and as such was unique in sixth-century Ireland. Here the male and female religious followed the same rule, shared the same church, and were jointly governed by the abbess and the bishop-abbot. A well-founded tradition has it that in both spiritual and temporal matters the lady abbess held 51% of the shares. And this seems only right if the tradition is to be believed that St Mel ordained Brigid a bishop.[24]

Irish society at the time of St Patrick and for centuries to follow was a familial one, having a socio-political structure with upwards of one hundred *tuaths* or statelets for perhaps half a million people. 'The term tuath,' says Professor O'Curry, 'was at the same time genealogical and geographical, having been applied to the people occupying a district which had complete political and legal administration.'[25] At the head of each tuath was the local king (*rí*); above him was the regional or provincial king and finally, at the very top, giving a broad based, loosely-defined unity to the entire island, was the High King (*Árd Rí*).

The king, whether local, provincial or national, was not the law-giver. Laws 'were adopted by the people in assembly (*oenach*), only the freemen having franchise.'[26] Irish traditional law, known as Brehon Law, is, 'the most archaic system of law and jurisprudence of Western Europe.'[27] Neither Roman nor Anglo-Saxon in origin, it had reached 'full proportions and maturity about the time that Alfred was reducing to order the scraps of elementary law he found existing among his people.'[28] Indeed, the system 'had sufficient vitality to remain in full force through all the vicissitudes of the country, even till many ages after the intrusion of the Anglo-Normans, in the twelfth century – who themselves indeed found it so just and comprehensive that they adopted it in preference to the laws of the countries from which they came.'[29]

Pre-Christian education in Ireland was the preserve of the numerous native schools of learning. 'The introduction of Christianity, and with it of the classical languages,' says Professor O'Curry, 'did not supersede the cultivation of the Gaelic... but on the contrary it appears to have encouraged and promoted it.'[30] Conflict there was between the new Latin and the old Gaelic, but it was not the conflict of the oppressor and the oppressed, for Christianity had come to illuminate rather than supplant.

Christian monasticism, with its stress on classical and biblical learning, flourished side by side with the native schools. Indeed, it is to the everlasting credit of the early monks that they were open enough and wise enough not only to tolerate the pagan schools but to incorporate and preserve in writing much of the native lore. The Celtic tradition in Europe is preserved in a large number of texts both of prose and poetry, of which the most important and valuable are those from Ireland. The monastic writer didn't necessarily subscribe to the sentiments expressed in the texts he was preserving but he had the largeness of heart to enable them to survive. The monk who preserved the text of the *Táin Bó Cuailnge* in the *Book of Leinster*, put in a plea for the accurate preservation and recounting of the saga. His final remark (in Latin) gives his assessment of what he has preserved: 'I who have written this story, or rather this fable, give no credence to the various incidents related in it. For some things in it are the deceptions of demons, others poetic figments; some are probable, others improbable; while still others are intended for the delectation of foolish men.'[31]

Early tensions between the school systems soon gave way to a spirit of mutual enrichment, though of course there were always those who were anti-intellectual or anti-classical or both. One ancient quatrain runs thus:

Is saoth liom an t-aos léinn
ag dul go hifreann pianach,
is an té nár léigh eagna
ag dul go parrthas grianach.

Sad to me that learned folk
adown to hell are going;
While he who read not wisdom
In sunny heaven is glowing.[32]

A late poem, attributed to St Colmcille, the darling of native and classical schools alike, bemoans the encroachments of Latin to the detriment of the native learning:

Beidh scoil gach cille de
ag lua léinn is Laidin,
gan fhios gan fhoras arubra
ach Laidin a luath-labhra.

The school of every church
Will cite learning and Latin,
No grasp of lore profound
Just speed in spewing Latin.[33]

And again:

Fólaim fealsúnachta is fás;
léann Gaeilge agus gluas,
litireacht léir agus ríomh,
is beag a mbín sa teach thuas.

Learning, philosophy are vain;
reading, grammar and gloss,
bookish learning and skill –
in heaven above are dross.[34]

Christianity adapted well to the social system and the cleric found a niche for himself among the *aes dana*, the men of special gifts, a highly organised professional class of druids, lawyers, doctors, historians and others. 'It is hard to resist the conclusion,' writes Myles Dillon, 'that the structure of the early church, with its emphasis on the local monastic community rather than on the diocese, was dictated by the political structure of the country; there would be considerable difficulty in the legal relationships of an ecclesiastical unit larger than a *tuath*.'[35]

Perhaps this modelling of the church on such a local basis, together with the warm personal attitudes of the Celts, fostered one of the deepest, if not the very deepest, and unique features of Christianity as it came to be developed in Ireland. That feature is *muintearas* (familiarity or community-mindedness). It is integral to the culture and repeatedly addressed in the religious and poetical tradition.

One of the models for understanding God was that of *rí* (king). In the *tuath*, however, the king was not a remote figure, an inaccessible personage in the mould of a mediaeval European monarch. The king was local – a neighbour's son, a man of the people. Even the *Árd Rí* (High King) was not really remote. 'When God is conceived on such a model,' says John Macquarrie, 'he cannot become too distant and likewise his creation cannot become so profane and godless as to arouse the acquisitive and aggressive spirit of irresponsible concupiscence.'[36] Prayer to God, therefore, was a cry from the heart, a tête-à-tête, rather than formal eloquence. The Martyrology of Oengus, dating from about AD 800, uses no less than six native Irish vocables and one loanword with reference to prayer. Warm, endearing expressions are common and perhaps the most popular name for Christ has always been 'Mac Muire', i.e. 'Mary's Son' or 'Son of Mary'.[37]

In the same vein the *Lúireach Phádraig*, alias, the *Lorica* or *Breastplate of Patrick*, captures the same intimate presence of the Lord. In part it runs:

Christ with me, Christ before me,
Christ behind me, Christ within me,
Christ beneath me, Christ above me,
Christ on my right, Christ on my left…
Christ in the heart of everyone who thinks of me,
Christ in the mouth of everyone who speaks to me,
Christ in every eye that sees me,
Christ in every ear that hears me.[38]

Perusal of typical Celtic poems and prayers show that this kind
of prayer is not unique to Patrick. Prayers of a similar style are
attributed to Brendan, Gildas, Fursa, and others. Prayers of protection, blessing, praise, are to be found for the widest variety of
human activity, be it getting up in the morning or going to bed
at night, and just about everything that happens in between – for
example, kindling the fire, going to Mass, going to work, and returning from same, seeing the moon, the change of year, change
of house, births, marriages and deaths. Every human activity or
state of being is an invitation to recognise the presence of God.

Likewise, the sense of God's immanence in his creation is a
marked feature of the spirituality of Early Christian Ireland.
Brendan Kennelly's happy translation of an ancient poem describes paradise as follows:

> Round the tree of Life the flowers
> Are ranged, abundant, even;
> Its crest on every side spreads out
> On the fields and plains of Heaven.
>
> Glorious flocks of singing birds
> Celebrate their truth,
> Green abounding branches bear
> Choicest leaves and fruit.
>
> The lovely flocks maintain their song
> In the changeless weather,
> A hundred feathers for every bird,
> A hundred tunes for every feather.[39]

A poem ascribed to Abbot Manchin Leith (who died in AD 665)
but probably dating from the ninth century, echoes the sentiments of thousands of Irish monks and anchorites of the Celtic
Church era:

> I wish, O Son of the living God,
> O ancient eternal King,
> for a hidden little hut in the wilderness,
> that it may be my dwelling.

An all-grey lithe little lark
to be by its side,
a clear pool to wash away sins
through the grace of the Holy Spirit.

Quite near,
a beautiful wood around it on every side,
to nurse many-voiced birds,
hiding it with its shelter.

A southern aspect for warmth,
a little brook across its floor,
a choice land with many gracious gifts
such as be good for every plant.

A few men of sense –
we will tell their number –
humble and obedient
to pray to the King...

A pleasant church and with the linen altar-cloth,
a dwelling for God from Heaven,
then,
a shining candle above the pure white Scriptures...
One house for all to go to for the care of the body,
without ribaldry,
without boasting,
without thought of evil.

This is the husbandry I would take,
I would choose and will not hide it:
fragrant leek, hens, salmon, trout,
bees.

Raiment and food enough for me
from the King of fair fame,
and I to be sitting for a while
praying God in every place.[40]

The nature poetry may seem romantic and idyllic, and in a sense it is, but the early Irish monks – and presumably everybody else as well – had a relationship with nature that was both practical and respectful. We know that Colmcille worked miracles, but never where simple good sense would suffice. Thus, he warned one of the brethren not to presume on God's providence by taking short cuts across the open sea to Tiree but to go the safer way by 'island-hopping'.

The love of nature and the spirit of gentleness was often conveyed with a touch of quaint humour. Keating records the following delightful story:

> Mochua and Colmcille were contemporaries, and when Mochua was a hermit in the desert the only cattle he had in the world were a cock and a mouse and a fly. The cock's service to him was to keep the matin time of midnight; and the mouse would let him sleep only five hours in the day-and-night, and when he desired to sleep longer, through being tired from making many crosses and genuflections, the mouse would come and rub his ear, and thus waken him; and the service the fly did him was to keep walking on every line of the Psalter that he read, and when he rested from reciting his psalms the fly rested on the line he left off at till he resumed the reciting of his psalms. Soon after that these three precious ones died, and Mochua, after that event, wrote a letter to Colmcille, who was in Í, in Alba (i.e., Iona in Scotland), and he complianed of the death of his flock. Colmcille wrote to him, and said thus: 'O brother,' said he, 'you must not be surprised at the death of the flock that you have lost, for misfortune exists only where there is wealth.'[41]

Indeed that spirit of utter detachment which Colmcille was hinting at was dear to the monk. He revelled in God's world, savoured it to the full, but always in a spirit of detachment knowing that everything was ultimately in the hands of God. It was said of St Brigid, for example, that her detachment was such that she

loved not the world:
She sat the perch of a bird on a cliff.[42]

With reference to the love of nature among the Celts, Kuno
Meyer writes:

> In Nature poetry the Gaelic muse may vie with that of any
> other nation. Indeed, these poems occupy a unique position
> in the literature of the world. To seek out and watch and love
> Nature, in its tiniest phenomena as in its grandest, was given
> to no people so early and so fully as to the Celt. Many hun-
> dreds of Gaelic and Welsh poems testify to this fact. It is a
> characteristic of these poems that in none of them do we get
> an elaborate or sustained description of any scene or scenery,
> but rather a succession of pictures and images which the
> poet, like an impressionist, calls up before us by light and
> skillful touches. Like the Japanese, the Celts were always
> quick to take an artistic hint; they avoid the obvious and the
> commonplace; the half-said thing to them is dearest.[43]

The love of nature among the early Irish saints, and their remark-
ably comfortable relationship with both tame and wild animals,
anticipates the Franciscan tradition by half a millennium.

That spirit of gentleness flowing from their Christianity is evident too in the warm homely words and images used of Christ
and of his mother Mary. A touching hymn to the infant Jesus is
attributed to St Íde, 'the foster-mother of the saints of Ireland,'
whose most famous disciple, Brendan, is reputed to have been
the discoverer of America in the sixth century. 'This is a most
tender and beautiful poem,' says Diarmuid Ó Laoghaire, SJ,
'rendered intimate by the use of several diminutives which unfortunately are untranslatable:

> Little Jesus [Íosagán]
> is nursed by me in my little hermitage.
> Though a cleric should have great wealth,
> all is deceit but little Jesus.
> The nursing [fostering] done by me in my house
> is not the nursing of one of low degree.
> Jesus with the people of heaven
> is by my heart every night...

The sons of nobles, the sons of kings,
although they come into my country,
not from them do I expect profit;
dearer to me is little Jesus...[44]

Besides a delight in the infancy of Jesus, there seems to have been
an intense compassion for Christ and Mary in their sufferings.
Several hundred years before the composition of the *Stabat
Mater*, Blathmac son of Cú Brettan, a monk and poet living about
AD 700, dedicates over a thousand lines of poetry to the passion
of 'Mary and her Son', and invites the mother of God to come
and share her grief with him:

Come to me, loving Mary,
that I may keen with your very dear one.
Alas that your son should go to the cross,
he was a great diadem, a beautiful hero...

When every outrage was committed against him,
when capture was completed,
he took his cross upon his back –
he did not cease being beaten.

The King of the seven holy heavens,
when his heart was pierced,
wine was spilled upon the pathways,
the blood of Christ flowing through his gleaming sides...

It would have been fitting for God's elements,
the beautiful sea,
the blue heavens, the present earth,
that they should change their aspect when keening their
hero...

The King was patient
at the crucifixion of his only-begotten,
for had his good elements known,
they would have keened sweetly...

Blathmac upbraids the Jews for shameless breach of kinship ties in putting Christ to death:

Of shameless countenance and wolf-like
were the men who perpetrated that kin-slaying;
since his mother was one of them
it was treachery towards a true kinsman.

But if the Jews were harsh towards 'Jesus, darling son of the virgin' there was sympathy in abundance for him from other sources:

Tame beasts, wild beasts, birds
had compassion on the Son of the living God;
and every beast that the ocean covers –
they all keened him.

Having keened the passion of Christ, Blathmac petitions Mary:

Let me have from you my three petitions,
beautiful Mary, little bright-necked one;
get them, sun of women,
from your son who has them in his power...

For you, bright Mary, I shall go as guarantor;
anyone who shall say the full keen shall have his reward.
I call you with true words, Mary, beautiful queen,
that we may hold converse together to pity your heart's darling.[45]

A poem ascribed to Colmcille, but probably a tenth-century composition, is in the traditional form of a litany:

Christ's cross over this face, and thus over my ear.
Christ's cross over this eye. Christ's cross over this nose.
Christ's cross over this mouth. Christ's cross over this throat.
Christ's cross over the back of this head. Christ's cross over this side.[46]

The author goes on to invoke the protection and blessing of

Christ's cross on the belly, the lower belly, the thighs, the legs, the arms and shoulders and 'from the top of my head to the nail of my foot,' as well as asking to have 'Christ's cross over my community. Christ's cross over my church.'[47]

A blessing before leaving on a journey – an eleventh century composition perhaps – combines the Trinitarian theme with that of the Virgin and her Son:

> May this journey be expeditious, may it be a journey of profit in my hands!
> Holy Christ against demons, against weapons, against slaughters!
>
> May Jesus and the Father, may the Holy Spirit sanctify us!
> May mysterious God that is not hidden in darkness, may the bright King save us!
>
> May the cross of Christ's body and Mary guard us on the road!
> May it not be unlucky for us! May it be prosperous, expeditious![48]

This prayer is also in the style of the *Lorica*. The prayer-form takes its origins from St Paul's image of putting on the spiritual armour of the Lord. It is a prayer of clothing oneself to do battle with the enemy. Hence the term *Lorica* (Breastplate). A fine example is the *Lorica* of St Fursa, a monk and bishop who went from the West of Ireland to Gaul in the sixth century and is still honoured at Péronne in Picardy – anciently known as *Perona Scottorum*, (Péronne of the Irish):

> The arms of God be around my shoulders,
> the touch of the Holy Spirit upon my head,
> the sign of Christ's cross upon my forehead,
> the sound of the Holy Spirit in my ears,
> the fragrance of the Holy Spirit in my nostrils,
> the vision of heaven's company in my eyes,
> the conversation of heaven's company on my lips,
> the work of God's church in my hands,

the service of God and the neighbour in my feet,
a home for God in my heart,
and to God, the Father of all, my entire being.[49]

Of the 'Lorica' type prayers Gougaud says:

These long enumerations of petitions, these series of adjura-
tions, ardent invocations, these enumerations of spiritual and
bodily dangers... the whole, divided by pious aspirations
pressing effusions towards God and the Saints, strong sentiments of repentance, compunction, of distrust of self, that is
what gives to these ancient Celtic prayers an appearance and
a very special quality.[50]

The love of Christ naturally led to love for neighbour and this
was aided in turn by a tradition of hospitality among the people
of the land even before the coming of Christianity. Of Finn
McCool, the pre-Christian folk hero, it was said:

Turn brown leaves to gold
On an autumn day,
Turn white waves to silver –
Finn would give all away.[51]

Lack of hospitality carried its own punishment – generally in the
form of disastrous reputation and sometimes an early grave.
Before Patrick's time, Eochaidh, a prince and hostage, managed
to escape from captivity. On being refused hospitality at a house
he had to go back home on an empty stomach. But as soon as he
had been adequately refreshed he returned with some followers
and proceeded to burn down the house and kill the son of the inhospitable householder.[52]

The Irish word for hospitality is *oigedchaire*, literally 'guest-lov-
ing.' In the Christian vision of life the guest was always Christ:

God in Heaven!
The door of my house will always be

Open to every traveller.
May Christ open His to me!

If you have a guest
And deny him anything in the house,
It's not the guest you hurt.
It's Christ you refuse.[53]

From another source we have the following dialogue:

Cuimmine: 'And what about the welcome of fire and bed?'
Comghan: 'It is the same as journeying to Rome on the way
of Paul and Peter.'[54]

And again:

Although fasting and prayer are good,
Although abstinence and fast are good,
better is it to bestow a thing
and keep one's mouth shut.[55]

Any form of inhospitable conduct is reprehensible, even in prayer. A prayer made for oneself alone is known in Irish as a *paidir ghann*, literally, a 'scarce prayer,' or 'stingy prayer'.

This same spirit of generosity to the point of prodigality characterised the people's response to the Christian message and accounts in large measure for the strikingly high numbers following the monastic calling in the new Irish church. Even in Patrick's own lifetime there was an extraordinary flowering of evangelical and religious life. Recounting a particular instance of it, he says:

There was, in particular, a virtuous Irish lady of noble birth and great beauty, already grown to womanhood. I had baptised her myself. A few days later she came to us with a problem on her mind. She had been advised, in a divine message, she said, to become a nun and thus to approach more nearly to God. Thanks be to God, six days later she carried out what he had proposed and dedicated herself with a fine enthusiasm to God. So, too, with other virgins. Their fathers disapprove of them, so they often suffer persecution and unfair abuse from their parents; yet their number goes on increasing. Indeed, the number of virgins from our converts is beyond counting, and to these must be added the widows and those who forego their marriage rites. Of them all the women who live in slavery suffer the most. They have to endure terror and threats all the time. But the Lord gives grace to many of his handmaids and although they are forbidden, they follow him courageously.[56]

The developing Irish monasticism had its own peculiar flavour. 'A sixth-century Irish monastery,' writes Tomás Ó Fiaich, 'must not be pictured like one of the great mediaeval monasteries on the Continent. It was much closer in appearance to the monastic settlements of the Nile valley or the island of Lerins than to later Monte Cassino or Clairvaux. Even the Latin word *monasterium* when borrowed into Irish under the form *muintir* was applied not to the buildings but to the community.'[57] Indeed it is typical that *muintir* should mean the household rather than the house, for the Celts were ever more interested in people than in institutions.

Daily routine in the monastery is succinctly stated by St Columbanus: 'Pray daily, fast daily, study daily, work daily.'[58] Daily prayer centred on the Divine Office. Eucharistic liturgy seems to have been reserved for Sundays and feasts, and by AD 800 the standard practice included Thursdays also. There was no uniformity or rigidity in celebrating either Mass or Office – a typical Celtic trait. 'Variety was not felt to endanger unity even in matters of faith.'[59]

Early Irish literature and manuscript materials abound with references to the divine services, especially the vigils and the night office of Matins, dear to the Irish not only because of a leaning towards the penitential, but also perhaps springing from the natural Irish characteristic of being people of the night. The little monastic bell which summoned all to prayer was indeed a sacramental of special significance. An eighth or early

ninth-century liturgical book introduces this marginal quatrain
as a grammatical illustration:

> The wind over the Hog's Back moans,
> It takes the trees and lays them low,
> And shivering monks o'er frozen stones
> To the twain hours of night-time go.[60]

Another monk consoles himself in his choice of a bell over a belle:

> I'd sooner keep my tryst
> With that sweet little bell
> The night of a bad winter mist
> Than risk a ravenous female.[61]

Yet another monk is having problems of concentration and cannot keep his mind on his Psalter:

> During the psalms they wander on a path that is not right;
> they run, they disturb, they misbehave before the eyes of
> great God.

> Through eager assemblies, through companies of giddy girls,
> through woods, through cities – swifter than the wind...

> Neither edged weapon nor the sound of whip-blows keeps
> them down firmly;
> they are as slippery as an eel's tail gliding out of my grasp...

> O beloved truly chaste Christ to whom every eye is clear,
> may the grace of the sevenfold Spirit come to keep and check
> them.[62]

The *Stowe Missal* (or *Tallaght Missal*) – an important manuscript
written in the monastery of Tallaght, Co Dublin, in the late
eighth or early ninth century – has interesting information on
the celebration of the Eucharist. As presented there the Liturgy
of the Mass contains a confession of sins, the recitation of the
litany of the saints, scripture readings, and numerous prayers.[63]
Drawing on Gougaud's research, John Ryan says that 'an exami-

nation of the different elements... shows that its affinities are with the church in Gaul, but that it has been influenced by the liturgies of Spain, Milan, and (above all) Rome.'[64]

The doctrine of the 'Communion of Saints' commends itself in a particular way to the Irish Celt because of the community bond or *muintearas* which knows no divide between the other world and this. *The Tallaght Missal* mentions twenty-four saints in the Eucharistic Prayer; the *Bobbio Missal* thirty-one. *The Antiphonary of Bangor* prays:

> May bishop Patrick pray for us all, that the sins we have committed may forthwith be blotted out... By the merits and prayers of St Comgall our Abbot, O Lord, preserve us all in your peace... Mindful of your triumphant martyrs, O God, have mercy on your people... O holy and glorious, wonderful and powerful martyrs, be mindful of us always in the sight of the Lord.'[65]

In the *Rule* attributed to Colmcille, monks are encouraged to pay their respects to their departed brothers by 'Fervour in singing the Office for the Dead, as if every faithful dead person was a friend of your own.'[66] Cummian's Penitential directs that Mass be offered for a dead monk on the day of the funeral and on the third day afterwards. And the dead in general are commemorated as follows in the Eucharistic Prayer from the *Bobio Missal*: 'Remember also, O Lord, the names of those who have gone before us with the sign of faith, and sleep in the sleep of peace... To these, and to all resting in Christ, grant, we beseech thee, a place of refreshment, light, and peace.'[67]

At prayer in general, standing was the usual posture adopted, but on solemn feasts the brethren were allowed to sit during part at least of the ceremonies. They showed an enviable enthusiasm in reciting the psalms and other vocal prayers – one Fiacc, having been baptised by Patrick, is reputed to have learned to read the Psalter in Latin in a matter of fifteen days.[68] The Sign of the Cross was made almost at every hand's turn. Patrick is said to have done so frequently. The *Rule* of St Columbanus required monks to use it in blessing their spoons, over their lamps when they lighted them, when walking, when going in or out, or on commencing work. Perhaps the tradition is rooted in Tertullian's warm words for that devotion: 'At every step, at every movement, when we go in or out; when we dress or put on our shoes, at the bath, at table; when lights are brought, when we retire to bed, when we sit down, whatever we do, we mark our foreheads with the sign of the Cross.'[69]

Genuflections and prostrations in phenomenal numbers were the order of the day – and of the night – in Irish ascetical practice. Oengus the Culdee is said to have made three hundred genuflections every night.[70] Though standing through most of the Eucharistic liturgy, the people prostrated themselves on the floor in absolute silence and reverence during the consecration.[71] A third posture at worship, that of kneeling with outstretched arms in the form of a cross, is most colourfully portrayed in the story of St Kevin of Glendalough who is said to have prayed so long with outstretched arms that the birds came and nested in the palms of his hands. Nor did he disturb them, says the legend, until the little ones had hatched out and flown away.

Ascetical practices constituted a significant expression of faith and 'it was hard to say whether Irish saints or Indian yogis practised the cruellest austerities.'[72] The *Féilire* or *Martyrology of Oengus the Culdee* is an interesting source of information on the various practices. Findchu, for example, used to lie the first night beside every corpse that was brought to his church for burial. Scothine expressed his understanding of penance and mortification by sleeping, not with one dead person, but with two live young ladies. (As a form of mortification, this practice has long since ceased in Ireland!) Colmcille, who died in AD 597, slept all alone in his bed; but then who would want to share the cold slab of stone on which he rested, and the pillow of stone whereon he laid his head? And if exotic sleeping patterns were not one's chosen penance, there was always flagellation. The *Féilire* mentions up to 280 instances of Oengus practising it.[73]

Fasting was a standard form of mortification. 'Fast daily,' said Columbanus. Fasting till later afternoon was practised on Wednesdays and Fridays throughout the year except from Easter to Pentecost. Forty days of fast were celebrated not once but three times in the year – forty days before Easter, forty before Christmas, and yet another forty ('the Fast of Elias') after Whitsuntide. St Aidan of Lindisfarne introduced the notion of fasting till the ninth hour (3 pm) on Wednesdays and Fridays. *The Annals of Loch Cé* have an entry under the year AD 1113 which reads, 'A thunderbolt fell on Crouching Aighle, on the night of the festival of Patrick, which destroyed thirty of the fasting people.'[74]

The *Bobbio Missal* in its Lenten Masses speaks of the omission to fast as sinful.[75] So central was this penitential practice that in the Irish enumeration of the days of the week, three of them – Wednesday, Thursday, and Friday – take their names from fasting habits: *Céadaoin* (Wednesday), literally, 'the first fast'; *An Aoine* (Friday), 'the fast'; and *Déardaoin* (Thursday), 'the day between the two fasts'. Amidst all the fasting, the Paschal Season stood out as a time of great joy and relaxation from mortifications. It has been called the 'Great Easter' – something comparable to heaven, an incentive to the monks to keep up the struggle and so come to the 'land of many melodies, musical, shouting for joy... feasting without extinction... partaking of the Great Easter.'[76]

Fasting in ancient Ireland belonged to the sphere of law as well as to that of religion.[77] Fasting against somebody as a means of gaining redress, exerting moral pressure, or cursing, was also common in ancient Ireland. There are examples of fasting on the land of the person one wishes to curse; of St Patrick fasting against a slave-owner to gain redress for the oppressed; and fasting even against God himself is not unknown as the following delightful anecdote from the *Féilire* testifies. The abbot of Dairinis once saw a little bird weeping and making great lamentation. 'O my God,' said the abbot, 'what has happened to that creature over there?' And with that he swore that he would neither eat nor drink until the cause be revealed to him. He had not long to fast, for an angel soon came that way and said, 'Hello Father! Don't let that question bother you any further. Molua, the son of Ocha, is dead. And he is mourned by the creatures for he never killed any of them, big or small. So he is mourned by them as much as by humans, and among those mourners is this little bird that you see.'[78]

Together with his injunction to pray daily and fast daily, Columbanus enjoined his monks to 'work daily.' Work on the land was necessary for maintaining a livelihood. As well as that there was art and craft work, such as metallurgy, monumental sculpture, and manuscript copying, all with their subsidiary support services. Far from rejecting pre-Christian art forms, the monasteries developed them to such peaks of refinement that survivals such as *The Book of Kells*, The Ardagh Chalice, and The Derrynaflan Altar Set are the admiration of the world.

Columbanus's fourth injunction, 'study daily' was so zealously followed that Ireland became renowned for scholarship. The scholar *par excellence* in Ireland was the scribe. The dignity and perfection of his art is an indication of the reverence accorded to sacred scripture, which so frequently formed the subject matter for his transcriptions. About *The Book of Kells*, for example, Alice Curtayne writes:

All the well-known patterns of Celtic art appear in the ornamentation: the dots around the capital letters, the interlaced bands, the vine and grape clusters, strutting peacocks, writhing serpents, biting animals – all combine with a lavish use of colour: crimson, blue, gold, green. The text, too, is varied by the use of scarlet and mauve inks.

The capital letters are lost in such a wealth of decoration that they are no longer legible; their identity is solved by the following script. This obscurity is said to have been deliberate, as a sort of protection against the profane. The capitals, in fact, are used rather like the rood screen before the altar, a kind of symbolic check interposed between the inner mysteries of the place of sacrifice and the multitude without. The capital letters are evidence of the tendency to mystification which is such a well-known trait of the Celtic mind – a tendency indeed omnipresent in the whole mysterious art.[79]

Still treating of *The Book of Kells,* Alice Curtayne continues:

The *Book of Kells* poses several questions. Does the prominence given to Our Lady confirm special veneration of her in the early Irish Church? Biblical experts have their own angle on the Book; historians and linguists have others. The de Paors, archaeologists, made a bold jump recently over what would at first sight seem an unbridgeable chasm and pointed out that James Joyce's *Finnegan's Wake* finds an antecedent in the *Book of Kells.* Joyce and the anonymous scribe had at least Celtic mystification in common.[80]

A host of monastic schools sprung up all over the country in the sixth and following centuries. They offered both sacred and secular learning, apparently without distinction of class or nationality. Indeed, there were so many Englishmen at school in Armagh that their part of the campus was known as 'The Saxon Third.'

Clonmacnoise on the Shannon, founded by St Ciarán probably in AD 545, became Ireland's most attractive educational centre. Affectionately known as 'Kieran's plain of crosses,' it is said to have had three thousand students in its heyday. The thirty-three-year-old founder died within a short time of founding, but the great monastic school flourished for over a thousand years until its suppression by Henry VIII in the sixteenth century. Some sense of the tradition and sanctity of this most hallowed spot is captured in an old Gaelic poem by the bard O'Gillain, finely but freely translated by T. W. Rolleston:

In a quiet watered land, a land of roses,
Stands St Kieran's city fair;
And the warriors of Erin in their famous generations
Slumber there.

There beneath the dewy hillside sleep the noblest
Of the clan of Conn,
Each below his stone with name in branching Ogham
And the sacred knot thereon.

There they laid to rest the seven Kings of Tara,
There the sons of Cairbre sleep –
Battle-banners of the Gael, that in Kieran's plain of crosses,
Now their final hosting keep.

And in Clonmacnoise they laid the men of Teffia,
And right many a lord of Breagh;
Deep the sod above Clan Creide and Clan Conaill,
Kind in hall and fierce in fray.

Many and many a son of Conn, the Hundred-Fighter,
In the red earth lies at rest;
Many a blue eye of Clan Colman the turf covers,
Many a swan-white breast.[81]

Classical learning too was vigorously promoted in the monastic
schools, so thoroughly indeed that Arsene Darmesteter, the dis-
tinguished French philologist and man of letters, could write:

> The classic tradition, to all appearances dead in Europe, burst
> out into full flower in the Island of Saints, and the
> Renaissance began in Ireland seven hundred years before it
> was known in Italy. During three centuries Ireland was the
> asylum of the higher learning which took sanctuary there
> from the uncultured states of Europe. At one time Armagh,
> the religious capital of Christian Ireland, was the metropolis
> of civilisation.[82]

With the collapse of the Roman Empire and the ensuing Dark
Ages, Ireland became a promised land. Bede, the great English
historian of the eighth century, speaks of nobility and common-
ers alike forsaking their native country either for the grace of
sacred learning or a more austere life in Ireland: 'And some of
them presently devoted themselves to the monastical life; others

chose rather to apply themselves to study, going about from one master's cell to another. The Scots [i.e. the Irish] willingly received them all, and took care to supply them with food, as also to furnish them with books to read, and their teaching, gratis.'[83] Of Bede's countrymen, Montalambert comments: 'The Anglo-Saxons, who were afterwards to repay this teaching with ingratitude so cruel, were of all nations the one which derived most profit from it.'[84]

Such was Ireland's reputation that when in neighbouring countries a studious person went missing, it was concluded that he had gone to Ireland to further his education. And in the days of Charles the Bald if anybody on the Continent professed to know Greek, he was deemed to be an Irishman, the pupil of an Irishman or a damn liar.[85] Both St Columbanus in the sixth century and Adomnán of Iona in the seventh show their thorough mastery of the Latin language and mention many classical authors, especially Virgil and Horace, in their writings, so that the claim that the Renaissance began in Ireland seven centuries ahead of Italy has solid foundations.

But the movement of people was not all in the direction of Ireland. Irish monks, who in all probability first went to the Continent to seek places of solitude, found themselves missionaries by accident, because their gospel-centred life blossomed into pastoral care for those among whom they lived. The exodus of monks from Ireland between the sixth and ninth centuries was phenomenal. 'Into the foreign lands these swarms of saints poured as though a flood had risen,' wrote St Bernard. 'Of these,' said he, 'one, St Columbanus, came to our Gallic lands and built a monastery at Luxeuil, and was made there a great people. So great a people was it, they say, that, choir following after choir, the divine office went on unceasingly and not a moment of day or night was empty of praise.'[86]

Columbanus himself, who died at his monastic foundation in Bobbio, Italy, in AD 615, was the most noted example of Irish scholarship in the Europe of his day. 'We need only to glance at his writings,' says the Celtic Scholar Jubainville, 'to be at once convinced of his wonderful superiority over St Gregory the Great and the Gallo-Roman scholars of his time.'[87] This restless, fearless, stormy and sainted intellectual has the foundation of more than a hundred monasteries directly or indirectly to his credit. Not only was he fearless in the face of the most powerful and wicked civil rulers, but his love for the Holy See drove him to rebuke the Pope himself, urging him not to become the tail of the church when he was its head, and adding, with an apology for his bluntness in addressing the Bishop of Rome, 'for amongst us [Irish] it is not a man's station but his principles that matter.'[88] The purity of his intention in admonishing the Holy Father is evident in the gracious conclusion to the letter: 'Farewell, sweetest Father in Christ, be mindful of us in your holy prayers when you are near the ashes of the saints.'[89]

The 'ashes of the saints' were precious from the earliest times in the universal church and Ireland was no exception. In his letter on the Paschal Controversy, St Cummian says that the delegates who went to Rome from the Synod of Old Leighlin in AD 630 returned with relics of the martyrs. After that same controversy, St Colman of Inis Boffin took the relics of St Aidan of Lindisfarne back to Ireland with him. In Viking times the relics of St Colmcille were moved back and forth between Iona and Ireland for safety, and right through Early Mediaeval times the relics of St Brigid drew large crowds to her monastic foundation at Kildare.

Reasons varied for going into exile from Ireland: some went in search of solitude, some went to do penance – possibly a penance imposed by a confessor – some went out of missionary zeal. But the principal motive for travelling abroad was to be on pilgrimage for Christ's sake. 'He set sail from Ireland for Britain,' says Adomnán of Colmcille, 'desiring to be a pilgrim for Christ.'[90]

The pain and sacrifice of Colmcille's leaving Ireland for love of Christ is beautifully expressed in Keating's *Mo Bheannacht Leat, a Scríbhinn*, a farewell poem attributed to him, and here translated from the Irish by Patrick Pearse:

My blessing with thee, writing,
To the delightful isle of Erin.
Alas, that I see not her hill-tops,
Tho' frequent blaze their beacons!

Farewell to her princes and people,
A fond farewell to her clerics,
Farewell to her gentle women,
Farewell to her learned in letters!

Farewell to her level plains,
A thousand farewells to her hills,
All hail to her that dwelleth there,
Farewell to her pools and lakes!

Farewell to her fruit-bearing forests,
Farewell to her fishing weirs,
Farewell to her bogs and leas,
Farewell to her raths and moors![91]

There are three kinds of pilgrimage, says the *Life* of Colmcille, in
the *Book of Lismore*:

(a) leaving one's country for love of God, and forsaking vice
for virtue;

(b) leaving one's country in body and with no change of
heart; from this, one derives 'neither fruit nor profit to the
soul;'

(c) having the *desire* to go on pilgrimage when the call of duty
demands a life at home.[92]

Perhaps a natural inclination to wander made pilgrimage con-
genial to the Irish. At any rate, at a time when most other people
moved no more than a league or two from their own front door,
the Irish found their way to Iceland, Greenland, North America,
and more accessible spots such as Rome, Jerusalem, Compostella
di Santiago and Kiev. In the ninth century Walahfrid Strabo, the
illustrious historian and abbot of Reichenau on Lake Constance,
remarked that 'their habit of going on pilgrimage has now be-

come second nature.'[93] Over the years Continental Europe became dotted with their shrines and churches. Many of these
were hugely popular, such as the shrines of St Frigidian in Lucca
(Italy), St Kilian at Wurzburg (Germany) and Fursa at Péronne
(France) – Péronne had a church dedicated to St Patrick from
about AD 700.[94]

The pilgrimage to Rome was the heart's desire of the Irish religious. The Lives of the Irish Saints paint a picture of continuous pilgrimage to Rome throughout the Early Middle Ages: Ibar
of Begire Island, Kieran of Saighir, Abban of Kilabban, Finbarr
of Cork, Nennidh from Derrylin, Tighernach of Clones, Finnian
of Moville, Fursa of Péronne, Canice of Kilkenny, together with
Fillan, Colman Elo, Cummian Fada, and others beyond number
accomplished the journey. Cumine was so well established in
Rome in the seventh century that

If anyone went across the sea,
To sojourn at the seat of Gregory,
If from Ireland,
He required no more than the mention of Cumine.[95]

St Molua once asked his superior for permission to go to the
Eternal City. The abbot had some reservations, but the good
Molua pushed his case with urgency, exclaiming 'unless I see
Rome I shall not live long'. Another monk is not quite so enthu-
siastic – perhaps he had had personal experience:

To go to Rome
Much labour, little profit:
The King you seek here
You won't find there
Unless you've got him in your pocket.[96]

Right through the Middle Ages the desire to go on pilgrimage
overseas was so strong that church authorities tried to dampen
the enthusiasm. In the *Life* of Samthann, abbess of Clonbroney
on the Meath-Longford border, we are told that a certain man,
Tairchellach, who had been a teacher, came to the virgin and

said: 'I prefer to postpone my studies and devote myself to prayer.' She replied: 'But what can stabilise your mind lest it wander if you neglect spiritual study?' The man said: 'I desire to travel oversees on pilgrimage.' She said to him : 'If you can't find God on this side of the sea, certainly let us go overseas. But since God is near to all who invoke him, there is no need to go overseas because you can arrive at the kingdom of heaven from any land.'[97]

From surviving manuscript material we can get a picture of these *peregrini* who 'live for us not merely as historical figures but as actual persons, restless wanderers, shameless beggars, men of deep personal religion, lovers of learning, graceful poets and original thinkers, representative of a civilisation where the standard of religion and learning was high, in the point of learning distinctly higher than the contemporary continental standard.'[98] Of this superior learning the Irish made no secret. The story is told of two Irishmen who came as merchants of wisdom to the court of Charlemagne and there advertised their 'merchandise': 'If anyone is desirous of wisdom let him come to us and buy, for we have it for sale.' 'No one among the Irish,' as Gerard Murphy points out, 'not even the gentle Sedulius himself, was backward in entitling himself a wise man, or a sophist.'[99]

Naturally the *peregrini* brought with them to the Continent the practices and traditions of home. Thus, for example, we find them spreading the practice of spiritual direction and private 'confession'. An old Irish proverb says that 'A person without a confessor (*anam-chara* or soul-friend) is a body without a head.' In the Lives of Colmcille, Columbanus, and Maelruain of Tallaght, examples of the importance of confessing are found. We find too the Celtic warmth and directness in prayer, as illustrated in a little quatrain composed for the safe arrival of one Dermot coming overseas to visit Sedulius. For his safety, Sedulius, 'the most poetically minded and the most skillful as a craftsman of the poets of his day,' prays:

> Christ, defend Dermot with thy shield, we pray;
> and with his companions may he come in joy to this city.
> Mayest thou be a powerful pilot in our ship, O Beloved One:
> without Thee, O all-powerful, nothing can prosper.[100]

Another characteristic of the home culture not lacking among the Irish on the Continent was the practice of satire. John Eriugena, the greatest philosopher in the seven centuries between Augustine and Aquinas, having fallen out with his good friend Hincmar of Rheims, satirised him thus:

> Here lies Hincmar, a greedy grasping ruffian.
> This one noble act did he do: he died.[101]

Again, when Eriugena and the King of the Franks sat on either side of a table where wine and wit abounded, Charles the Bald quipped at the expense of the Irishman: 'What distinguishes a sot from a Scot (i.e. an Irishman)?' John shot back 'Only a table!'[102]

In its missionary and scholarly endeavours, the Early Irish Church was not preoccupied with detail in the matter of organised and structured apostolate. In this lay its strength and weakness both at home and abroad. It preserved the *human touch*, the warmth, the intimacy, the personal, but the price paid was a certain lack of a structuring which might have made for greater permanence. This is typically Celtic. Still, of its missionary endeavours at home and abroad, Professor Zimmer of the University of Berlin, in *The Irish Element in Mediaeval Culture* says:

> Ireland can indeed lay claim to a great past; she can not only boast of having been the birthplace and abode of high culture in the fifth and sixth centuries... but also of having made strenuous efforts in the seventh and up to the tenth century to spread her learning among the German and Romance peoples, thus forming the actual foundation of our present continental civilisation.[103]

But in its weaker aspect, in that lack of enduring organisation – if that indeed be weakness – another aspect of the Celtic mentality was revealed, namely, a preoccupation with mystery and the other world, a sensitivity to the transience of life, a feeling that 'we have not here a lasting city'. Of this Prionsias Mac Cana writes:

In all the vast range of traditional material handled by the monastic scribes and literati nothing seems to have captured their imagination quite so completely as the theme of the voyage to the happy other-world... Françoise Henry in her monumental study of Irish Art has drawn a sensitive and revealing comparison between the accounts of the voyage to the otherworld and the complex, elusive ornament of Celtic art. She finds both characterised by the same aversion to rigidity and to barren realism and she sees in the illuminated pages of the Gospel books the artistic reflex of the polymorphic otherworld: 'This multiform and changing world where nothing is what it appears to be is but the plastic equivalent of that country of all wonders which haunts the mind of the Irish poet, and in which all those impossible fancies seem to come true to which the world does not lend itself.[104]

I have chosen a poem from the eleventh century as a suitable ending to this chapter since that century saw the last stages of the 'Celtic Church.' The author, Mael Ísu Ua Brolcháin (d. 1086), fittingly expresses himself in the twin languages of that church: Gaelic and Latin. It is a song of longing, a cry from the heart for the one thing necessary: love of God. A translation of the original, preserving the metre, has been made by Dr George Sigerson, while the late Seán Óg Ó Tuama has composed for it a singularly appropriate melody which seamlessly mingles the musical styles of traditional Irish and plain chant. Ua Brolcháin's first stanza goes:

Deus meus, adiuva me!
Tuc dam do sheirc, a meic dil Dé.
Tuc dam do sheirc, a meic dil Dé
Deus meus, adiuva me!

Sigerson translates as follows:

Deus meus adiuva me (My God, assist Thou me),
Give me Thy love O Christ, I pray,
Give me Thy love O Christ, I pray,
Deus meus adiuva me.

In meum cor ut sanum sit (into my heart that it whole may be),
Pour loving King, Thy love in it,
Pour loving King, Thy love in it,
In meum cor ut sanum sit.

Domine, da quod peto a te (Lord, grant Thou what I ask of
Thee),
O pure bright sun, give, give, today,
O, pure bright sun, give, give today,
Domine, da quod peto a te.

Hanc spero rem et quaero quam (This thing I hope and seek
of Thee),
Thy love to have where'er I am,
Thy love to have where'er I am,
Hanc spero rem et quaero quam.

Tuum amorem sicut vis (Thy love as Thou mayest will),
Give to me swiftly, strongly, this,
Give to me swiftly, strongly, this,
Tuum amorem sicut vis.

Quaero, postulo, peto a te (I seek, I claim, and I ask of Thee),
That I in heaven, dear Christ, may stay,
That I in heaven, dear Christ, may stay,
Quaero, postulo, peto a te.

Domine, Domine, exaudi me (Lord, Lord, hearken to me),
Fill my soul, Lord, with Thy love's ray,
Fill my soul, Lord, with Thy love's ray,
Domine, Domine, exaudi me.

Deus meus adiuva me,
Deus meus adiuva me.[105]

CHAPTER 2

The Late Mediaeval Period

What is frequently referred to as the *Celtic* or *Pre-Norman* church in Ireland dates roughly from the coming of St Patrick in the fifth century to the coming of the Normans in the twelfth. Within that period, the seventh to the ninth centuries are designated *The Golden Age*, an age which was harshly, if gradually, terminated by the Viking raids which bedevilled Irish monasteries from the end of the eighth century and posed a continuing threat over the next two hundred years. Nevertheless, we find in the Irish church at the end of the eleventh and the beginning of the twelfth century sufficient vitality for a programme of self-reformation to be initiated. That reform was called for is scarcely to be doubted. Among other things, deeds of violence were frequent, not only against the people at large but also against people and places enjoying a degree of exemption – women, clergy, religious – and against church property. All of this was in breach of the age-old tradition recorded in the *Féilire*:

> Now these are the four laws of Érin:
> Patrick's law, not to kill the clerics;
> and Adomnán's law, not to kill women:
> Daire's law, not to kill cattle;
> and the law of Sunday, not to transgress [thereon].[1]

Nevertheless, native learning flourished and the metalwork, architecture and manuscript illumination of the time demonstrate the assimilation of many Viking, Roman, Gothic and other foreign elements into the mainstream of Irish artistry. Demand for manuscripts was great and the scribe, as in the days of old, applied himself to his skilled and disciplined task. The tedium of work in the scriptorium must have wearied more than the anonymous author who left on the margin of his manuscript a window into his world:

My hand is weary with writing;
my sharp great point is not thick;
my slender-beaked pen juts forth a beetle-hued
draught of bright blue ink.

A steady stream of wisdom springs
from my well-coloured neat fair hand;
on the page it pours its draught of ink
of the green-skinned holly.

I send my little dripping pen unceasingly
over an assemblage of books of great beauty,
to enrich the possessions of men of art –
whence my hand is weary with writing.[2]

A trend to give the Irish language a more prominent place than Latin developed in the tenth and continued through the following centuries, while the effort to replenish libraries after the Viking destruction made both the copying of manuscripts and the importation of books a high priority. With a decline in the monastic schools, increasing numbers of private families took it upon themselves to preserve a learned tradition in literature, and sufficient manuscripts have survived from the twelfth and following centuries to testify to an energetic pursuit of poetry, storytelling, law, philosophy and medicine.[3] Two further subjects dear to this intellectual *élite* were history and devotional literature. Both of these are of special interest to us in this work.

The High Middle Ages was a turning point in Irish history. At the beginning of the eleventh century Brian Boru, the head of a North Munster tribe, won his way to the high-kingship of Ireland and in doing so broke the mould of Irish politics and paved the way for a centralised monarchy as in the nation-states which evolved across Europe in the High and Late Middle Ages.

At the Battle of Clontarf (AD 1014) he defeated the Vikings and thereafter their power began to wane across Europe.

Also in the eleventh century, Irish pilgrims and missionaries to the Continent developed an awareness of how their own church organisation and practice differed from that of the Continent. Towards the end of the century reform was in the air, in some quarters at least, influenced by the reform and development that were taking place on Continental Europe.

Though by no means the only major agents in twelfth-century reform, the two people who came to personify it were St Celsus (Cellach) and St Malachy. At the beginning of the twelfth century, in 1105, Cellach succeeded to the abbacy of Armagh. Like so many of his ancestors and predecessors who held the office of *coarb* (successor) of Patrick, Cellach was a layman. Because he belonged to a party of reform he broke with the social convention of the day, got himself ordained both priest and bishop, and pushed forward vigorously with a reform of the church in Ireland. After his day, his nephew, Malachy, energetically advanced the ideals pursued by Cellach. The reforming activity of these two prelates covered most of the first half of the century and its momentum continued after Malachy's death in 1148.

In AD 1111, a national Synod was held at Raith Breasail, a place of uncertain identity, but thought to have been located near Cashel, Co Tipperary. Presiding over it were Cellach and the High King. Gilbert (*Gilla Espaic*), the Norse bishop of Limerick, and papal legate to the synod, introduced revolution ary plans for a parochial and diocesan structure for Ireland. His much-needed Norse organisational ability also led him to advance the concept of uniformity in the liturgy. Two ecclesiastical provinces were established following the old two-fold division of the country into upper and lower halves, with twelve dioceses in each.

The old monasteries and their schools were still in existence but, for the first time in its history, Ireland came to be administered by a diocesan system parallel to that on the mainland of Europe. A church based solely on the monastic system left much to be desired in the field of pastoral care. More balance between a monastic and a diocesan structure was needed.

Cellach died while visiting Munster in 1129. His death, wake and funeral are recorded in the *Annals of Loch Cé*:

> Cellach, coarb of Patrick, i.e. the chief bishop of the West of Europe; a pure, illustrious virgin; the only head whom Foreigners and Gaeidhel , *both* laics and clerics, obeyed, after having, moreover, ordained bishops and priests, and persons of every degree besides; and after having consecrated very many churches and cemeteries; after having bestowed jewels and wealth; and after having imposed faith and good manners on all, both laity and clergy; and after a life of Mass-celebration, fasting, *and* praying, and after unction and choice penance, resigned his soul into the bosom of angels and archangels, in Árd-Patraic, in Mumha, [Ardpatrick, Co Limerick] on the kalends of April, the 2nd (feria), in the twenty-fourth year of his abbotship, and in the fiftieth year of his age. His body was conveyed, truly, on the 3rd of the nones of April, to Lis-mor-Mochuda, [Lismore, Co Waterford] according to his own will; and it was waked with psalms, and hymns, and canticles, and was honourably interred in the tomb of the bishops on the day before the nones of April on the 5th feria [i.e. Thursday, April 5th].[4]

Cellach's successor, Malachy of Armagh, was a man of the same calibre as his uncle, and pushed ahead with the reform. The structuring of a diocesan system begun at Raith Breasail was brought to a successful conclusion at the Synod of Kells in 1152, and with few modifications has survived to the present day. Though death had come to Malachy shortly before the Synod, the success of the assembly was, in large measure, due to him, just as the success of Raith Breasail had been due to his uncle.

St Bernard of Clairvaux was a personal friend of Malachy, and when the latter died at Bernard's monastery in Champagne in 1148, Bernard wrote his *Life*. It is obvious, however, that Bernard indulged in hyperbole when compiling an inventory of the evils of Ireland in the days of his saintly friend:

When he began to administer his office, the man of God
[Malachy] understood that he had been sent not to men, but
to beasts... never had he found men so shameless in their
morals, so wild in their rites, so impious in their faith, so barbarous in their laws, so stubborn in discipline, so unclean in
their life. They were Christians in name, in fact they were pa-
gans.[5]

Though guilty on some of these counts, Ireland cannot have
been as bad as Bernard claims if it produced people of the calibre of Malachy himself whose person, spirit and general dispo-
sition so patently captivated the saint of Clairvaux. Bernard,
who had been brought up in a tradition of Roman law, was
quick to see any other legal system as barbarous, but the 'Celtic
Church' in Ireland had shown enough independence of spirit to
adopt Christianity without exchanging the Brehon Law for the
Roman code. At any rate, according to Bernard, his friend
Malachy got to work in traditional Irish style and spent 'entire
nights in vigil, holding up his hands in prayer,'[6] with the result
that,

Barbarous laws disappeared, Roman laws were introduced:
everywhere ecclesiastical customs were received and the
contrary rejected: churches were rebuilt and a clergy ap-
pointed to them: the sacraments were duly solemnised, and
confessions were made: the people came to church, and those
who were living in concubinage were united in lawful wed-
lock. In short all things were so changed that the word of the
Lord may today be applied to this people: 'those who before
were not my people are now my people'.[7]

One of the sources of friction during the work of reform was the
tension that existed between the native Irish church and the
newly established Hiberno-Norse sees which gave allegiance to
Canterbury. During the Viking period the Norse gained a
foothold on the coast and established a number of towns and
trading ports. Chief among these were Dublin, Waterford, and
Limerick. In time, the Norse became firmly established in the

Christian faith, but their culture was not Gaelic and their con-
nections were with foreign parts, England in particular, rather
than with the island on which they lived. In matters religious
they looked to Canterbury rather than Armagh. Malchus, the
first Bishop of Waterford (1096-1135), was a monk of
Winchester. It is not certain when Donatus was consecrated first
Bishop of Dublin, but it is probable that it took place about 1028
when Sitrick, the Norse king of Dublin, went to Rome on pilgrimage and contributed to Peter's Pence. Where and by whom
Donatus was consecrated we do not know, but we do know that
his successor, Patrick, was consecrated at Canterbury, and that
Malchus of Waterford was consecrated by St Anselm in
Canterbury. Both Anselm and his predecessor, Lanfranc, laid
claim to the primacy of Ireland; but as the reform progressed
problems were gradually resolved, and the connection between
the Norse-Irish and Canterbury was quietly dissolved in 1140.
This separation from Canterbury was further reinforced some
years later, when Cardinal Paparo arrived from Rome as legate
to the Synod of Kells and raised Tuam and Dublin to the level of
archbishoprics.

The other key event which makes the twelfth century memo-
rable in the annals of Ireland is the Norman Invasion in 1169.
The Norman-French knights had neither literary nor scholarly
interests. War and conquest, military advancement and social
organisation were their priorities. Within a century two-thirds
of the country was in their hands, but by then they had passed
their zenith and were already on retreat before the recovering
Gaelic nobility. Nevertheless, a host of Norman-French names
were to become part of the Irish scene; and Gaelic culture, manners, law, dress and speech were to be adopted by such prominent invading families as the FitzGeralds of Desmond and
Kildare, the Butlers of Ormond and the de Burgos of Connacht.
So thoroughly did they adopt the Irish way of life that they were
said to be *Hibernicis ipsis Hiberniores* 'more Irish than the Irish
themselves,'[8] but, as professor Brian Ó Cuív points out, 'this claim
was exaggerated. Though the Norman lords might appear to be

Irish princes, they did not renounce their emotional attachment to the English Crown'.[9] Such an attachment was meaningless to a native Irish person. Thus the cleavage remained.

The wars, feuds, squabbles and multiplicity of assassinations perpetrated by Norman on Norman, and on Norman by Irish and vice versa, were a matter for bitter lamentation by the annalists during the two centuries which followed the invasion. Little wonder then that in 1381 Richard Wye, Bishop of Cloyne, Co Cork, took unliturgical advantage of a requiem Mass which he was celebrating in Dublin Castle on the occasion of the death of Philippa, Countess of March, and 'did after beginning the accustomed preface introduce the words':

Eternal God,
there are two in Munster
who destroy us and what is ours.
These are the Earl of Ormond
and the Earl of Desmond
with those who follow them,
whom in the end the Lord will destroy
through Christ, our Lord.
Amen.[10]

Proceedings against Wye were set in motion. He was accused of slander, schism, and heresy, and consequently lost his diocese; but anybody reading the history of the times can well appreciate the exasperation of the bishop who 'with high voice said and sang these damnable words'.[11]

In the continuing unrest caused by the Norman Invasion, the Irish church suffered severely. For one thing, the old monastic schools broke down and no modern university on the lines of Paris, Bologna or Oxford rose to replace them. To say that the Irish were without high education would be untrue, but it was haphazard, fragmented, and ineffectual. Furthermore, political conflict and division were not confined to the secular world: the new religious orders – Franciscans, Dominicans, Cistercians, Augustinians, and others – were in a state of continual turmoil due to inter-racial strife.

Through Malachy's personal friendship with St Bernard, the Cistercians were introduced into Ireland in 1142. The Benedictines had established themselves some years earlier and many more emerging Continental orders were soon to follow. The Canons Regular of St Augustine, introduced by St Malachy, and later by St Laurence O'Toole, supplanted many of the Early Christian monastic foundations. The invading Normans brought with them monks from several orders on the Continent as well as from England, and established rival monasteries even of the same orders, as well as attempting to gain control of the existing Irish houses. This extension of the conquest to monastic precincts led to continual apartheid, gerrymander, and political jockeying, which more than once erupted in bloodshed and even in massacre. At the 1291 Franciscan chapter in Cork, for example, the sons of the gentle St Francis decided that action speaks louder than words, with the result that at the end of one plenary session the chapter-hall was strewn with the dead bodies of sixteen delegates. 'The enmity grew so fierce that in the early fourteenth century one Brother Simon declared solemnly that it was not a sin to kill an Irishman and, if he himself did such a deed, he would not on that account refrain from celebrating Mass.'[12] In an atmosphere of such acrimony there was little likelihood of genuine progress. How Ireland might have evolved schools of philosophy, theology and spirituality, had the Normans not invaded, is for ever a matter of conjecture.

The great codices and lesser manuscripts which were written in Irish and have survived the ravages of the centuries tell us much about the life, spirit, and spirituality of the people between the twelfth and the sixteenth century. Again and again we find old themes recurring, old attitudes surviving: pilgrimage, asceticism, fasting, alms-giving, hospitality, devotions – both native and foreign – to Christ in his passion , to Mary and to the saints, and in relation to the after-life. All of these and more besides were part and parcel of the furniture of Irish Christianity.

'The principal positive achievement of the feudal regime in Ireland,' writes Eoin MacNeill, 'was the development of town life... The early Irish laws take no cognisance of town communities... At all events, in Irish records, the first towns are monastic and academic centres, such as Armagh, Derry, Kildare, Cork. The first fortified towns were established by the Norsemen, and they soon became emporia of trade, chief among them being Dublin, Waterford and Limerick... Many of the towns under the feudal regime grew out of older monastic centres, but they became settlements of newcomers. The natural opposition between townsmen and feudal magnates caused the towns to rally to the monarchy and look to it for support. The monarchy in turn favoured the towns, which were the best source of revenue, supplies and transport by land and sea.'[13]

One of the benefits to stem from the existence of these towns and their improved shipping facilities was an increase in the number of foreign pilgrimages. Rome, Jerusalem, and Compostella were the most popular destinations outside of the country. Jubilee years in Rome drew exceptionally large numbers of pilgrims from Ireland. The pilgrimage to Colmcille's Island of Iona off the western coast of Scotland retained its popularity as a place of pilgrimage in mediaeval times. And at home, the annalists mention a plethora of pilgrim destinations for the purposes of prayer and repentance, for example, Clonmacnoise, Glendalough, Croagh Patrick, and Lough Derg.

Perhaps at this point it might be well to single out for more detailed consideration the most famous of all pilgrim sites in Ireland, St Patrick's Purgatory, Lough Derg. The fame and fortune of this pilgrimage is of considerable interest. Situated on a tiny lake-island in Co Donegal, St Patrick's Purgatory has been associated with the national patron from time immemorial. Though occasionally challenged, the tradition is soundly authentic that the saint did spend time in prayer and penance either on the island itself or in its vicinity. Before his coming, the spot may well have been the site of a pagan shrine, because tradition asserts the presence of a monstrous and extremely ill-be-

haved serpent in the lake. The tale giving the derivation of the
name Lough Derg tells how it was called Finnlough (the fair
lake) until Patrick, having prayed and cast his crozier at the serpent, so wounded it that the profusion of blood turned the lake
red. Thus the saint decreed that *the fair lake* be known thence till
Judgment Day as Lough Derg (the red lake).

The earliest written material available on the subject of the
Lough Derg Pilgrimage is from Henry of Saltrey, an English
Benedictine from Huntingdonshire, who, around 1152, wrote a
treatise *Concerning St Patrick's Purgatory*. According to Henry's
informant, a soldier who made the pilgrimage, the most trau-
matic aspect of it was making one's way through a cave on the
island. The cave itself is the real 'purgatory' where St Patrick, it
is said, prayed and did penance In that cave, the pilgrim is
expected to encounter a motley variety of other-world personalities from all known centres of population in that land of mystery. It was a harrowing experience and for this reason people
were recommended not to enter the cave at all. However, if they
insisted, a protocol for proceeding was well defined:

It was necessary in the first place to get the permission of the
bishop by letter addressed to the Prior [of the community
who served the place of pilgrimage] and the bishop always
dissuaded the pilgrim from attempting it. Having presented
the bishop's letter to the Prior, the latter also dissuaded the
adventurous individual, but if he persisted in his purpose, he
had to remain five days in retreat; then a Requiem Mass was
celebrated, at which he received the Holy Communion, and
he finally made his will. After these somewhat terrifying pre-
liminaries, if he was still determined to visit the cavern, the
clergy, in solemn procession, accompanied him to the pit's
mouth, singing the litanies, the Prior unlocked the door, the
adventurer took holy water, signed himself with the sign of
the Cross, and entered the cave, which was closed after him.
Next day the clergy went again to the pit's mouth; if there
was no appearance of the pilgrim, he was given up for lost,
but if he did appear, he was taken out, the clergy with great

joy conducted him to the church, where he spent fifteen days more in thanksgiving for his deliverance, which was almost regarded as a mark of predestination.[14]

So famous was the pilgrimage on the Continent that illustrious people flocked to it from all over Europe – Hungary, Italy, Rhodes, Spain, France, the Netherlands, England. Three metrical versions of Henry of Saltrey's story were published in the thirteenth century, followed by one in the fourteenth and another in the fifteenth. The thirteenth-century versions were published in French, the other two in English.

A cool and clinical Dutchman visited the shrine in the fifteenth century. On being asked for some contribution of a financial nature, and not realising that there might be some truth in the remark that the Irish are a 'nation of poets prone to believe in fables,'[15] he went hotfoot to Rome and informed Pope Alexander VI that the whole business was a money-making racket. Alexander duly issued a brief ordering the suppression of the pilgrimage and the destruction of the cave 'because it was an occasion of base avarice'.[16] If the truth were told, the same Alexander Borgia might well have derived a considerable and much needed spiritual uplift from a trip to Lough Derg. Be that as it may, his orders were carried out on St Patrick's Day, March 17th, 1497: the cave was destroyed and the pilgrimage suppressed.

Happily, and to the surprise of nobody, the pilgrimage soon revived and a new cave or 'prison' was constructed. Peter Lombard (d. 1620) described it as 'a narrow building roofed with stone which could contain twelve, or at most fourteen, persons kneeling two-and-two. There was a small window, near which those were placed who were bound to read the Breviary.'[17] Tadhg Dall Ó hUiginn, the sixteenth century Gaelic poet, refers to the cave as 'a haven to cleanse the soul from torment, bright Rome of the west of the world.'[18] Tadhg Dall, who probably went on pilgrimage himself, speaks of the healing properties associated with the Lough Derg pilgrimage:

Without, on the far side of the cave, is a pool to wash all from
their wounds, a shining smooth-banked lake-spring.
No wound, however grievous, was ever dipped neath the
wide,
spreading pool, the bright-pooled, dry, clear, warm, stream
that it would not bring out of it hail.[19]

Henry of Saltrey's informant described in some detail his tour of
the world beyond the grave, thus drawing upon himself and his
story the scorn of the above mentioned Dutchman. His story
nonetheless struck a familiar note with the Irish who felt as
much at ease in the other world as in this. So much so that a special category of Irish folk-tales entitled *echtrae* (adventure) have
as their chief motif the other world, known variously as The
Promised Land, The Land of the Living, The Delightful Plain,
The Many-coloured Land, and The Land of the Young (*Tír na
nÓg*), this last ascription being perhaps the most popular of all.
In the words of Myles Dillon:

> Here is introduced most strongly the Celtic magic, the imagi-
> native quality for which Irish literature is well known... The
> Irish Other World is a country where there is neither sickness
> nor age nor death; where happiness lasts forever and there is
> no satiety; where food an drink do not diminish when con-
> sumed; where to wish for something is to possess it; where a
> hundred years is as one day. It is the Elysium, the Island of
> the Hesperides of the Greeks; the Odains-Akr, the Jord
> Lifanda Manna, of the Norse. Alfred Nutt pointed out that it
> finds its closest analogues in early Greek mythology, and he
> suggests that it represents ancient Indo-European tradition.[20]

In the late mediaeval period, the old love of nature continued to
assert itself. The Colloquy of the Ancients (*Agallamh na
Seanórach*), a twelfth-century work purporting to be a dialogue
between St Patrick and a pre-Christian folk-hero named Caílte,
demonstrates the survival of the nature-loving spirit. 'Well,
Caílte, my soul,' said Patrick, 'what was the best hunting that

the Fenians ever had in Ireland or in Scotland?' 'The hunting of
Arran,' said Caílte. 'Where is that?' said Patrick. 'Between
Scotland and Pictland,' said Caílte, 'and we used to go there
with three companies of the Fianna on Lammas Day, and we
would get plenty of hunting there until the cuckoo called from
the tree-tops in Ireland. And sweeter it was than any music to
hear the cry of the birds there, as they rose from the waves and
coasts of the island. Thrice fifty flocks of birds frequented it, of
every colour, blue and green and grey and yellow.' And Caílte
sang a lay:

> *Arann na n-oigheadh n-iomdha*
> *Tadhal fairrge re a formna;*
> *Oileán i mbiadhtar buidhne,*
> *Druimne i ndeargtar gaoi gorma. etc.*

Arran of the many stags,
The sea strikes against its shoulder,
Isle where companies are fed,
Ridge on which blue spears are reddened.

Skittish deer are on her peaks,
Delicious berries on her manes,
Cool water in her rivers,
Mast upon her dun oaks.

Greyhounds are there and beagles,
Blackberries and sloes of the dark blackthorn,
Her dwellings close against the woods,
Deer scattered about her oak-woods.

Gleaning of purple upon her rocks,
Faultless grass upon her slopes,
Over her hair shapely crags
Noise of dappled fawns a-skipping.

Smooth is her level land, fat are her swine,
Bright are her fields,
Her nuts upon the tops of her hazel-wood,
Long galleys sailing past her.

Delightful it is when the fair season comes;
Trout under the brinks of her rivers,
Seagulls answer each other round her white cliff,
Delightful at all times is Arran![21]

The person of Christ, particularly in his passion and cross, was
still central to Irish spirituality in the high and late mediaeval
period, as was devotion and love for his mother Mary. In the
Irish as in the Orthodox tradition, one does not separate mother
and son.

Christ's crucifixion for our sake is spoken of in terms borrowed from the Brehon Laws as the payment of the *eric* or
blood-fine. The poems of the thirteenth century author,
Donnchadh Mór Ó Dálaigh, include two interesting works on
the cross in which the mediaeval legends of its origin from the
Tree of Paradise are used. 'These are fine poems in their way,'
says Eleanor Knott, 'not unfit to be compared in some measure
with some of the well-known Latin pieces on the same theme.'[22]
Knott goes on to quote a translation (from the Irish) of the open-
ing lines of one piece:

A beacon to the world is the holy Cross,
conspicuous tree of fair brown surfaces;
roads that are the brightest to look on
are the seals of this tree of the five wounds.
The cross of Jesus, relic which gives succour to all;
many are the kinds in which the golden-comely bright dry
supple one
from the fair seed of the wood of paradise is called a beacon...
From its side came the light that dispersed the darkness of
this world;
it is not a beacon unworthy of trust,
that which drowned [i.e. expunged] the Lord's original claim
[i.e. freed repentant man from the consequences of the
Fall].[23]

When Geoffry Fionn Ó Dalaigh's young son Eoghan died, his father composed a mystical poem apostrophising the cross which reminds him both of the loss of his son and the Cross of Jesus:

> It is you, O cross of the merry lad,
> that has made me cheerless this night;
> O firm cross by which I sorrow,
> 'tis you shall quench my happiness...
> The cross that has grieved me
> is shaped like yours, O Lord;
> because of it
> may he whose cross it is come to your house.
> To shelter by Eoghan's cross
> will release my sorrow again,
> a protection from an army it is,
> and yet, O God, it is no protection from grief.[24]

Richard Butler, a fifteenth century Anglo-Norman, tested his skill at Gaelic bardic metre, and while he did not quite master the technicalities, he captured something more valuable: the sincerity of a traditional Irish prayer:

> May the King of the Sunday, my doctor,
> And Mary, my physician in my illness –
> And the holy Cross – grant, that without too great sorrow
> I shall be parted from my illness.[25]

A summary of topics treated by the bardic poets of the late middle ages is given by Peter O'Dwyer as: 'the mystery of the Trinity, Creation, the Annunciation, the Incarnation and Infancy, the Passion, the Cross, the Crucifixion, the Wounds, especially the piercing of the side with the spear, His Descent into hell, Mary, judgment, heaven, sin and repentance, the angels and saints.'[26]

Donnchadh Mór Ó Dálaigh (d. 1224), one of the outstanding poets of the age, having written many poems of a more or less secular nature, thinks it fitting to pay a tithe on his talent. He applies Brehon Law, rather than the Pauline theology of the Mystical Body, to establish his claim of brotherhood with Christ:

May the son of you, my sister,
Bring me safely through life –
Though I do not deserve a good end –
You from whose breast he drank your substance.

The Lord who formed me
Must look mercifully on me;
After all, He is my brother
Since I have the good mother of God for a sister.[27]

A sixteenth century poet living in exile in Scotland, sings the praises of Mary and appeals for her protection at the Judgment, an event which, in Irish tradition, is due to take place on a Monday:

As I dread that on the Monday of the Tribute – a hard case – the Red Cross and the death of Jesus will confront me, beguile thy Christ on that day.[28]

Though the theology of the poet sounds strange to us today, it was typical among the poets of the time and presumably among the preachers.[29] In the same poem, the author adds a lovely human touch when he grieves with Mary in her sorry lot as her son is in the tomb:

The Virgin Mary suffered as much as the passion...
while God's Son was in the grave after it,
and her cheeks red as embers.[30]

Titles of honour and comments on Mary's physical beauty abound through the rest of the poem: 'O harp of tuneful strings', 'O cheek of the hue of the berry', 'O smiling face', 'O protecting shield', 'O mighty soil of virtue', etc.[31] Such title-giving was normal practice among Gaelic writers of all ages.

The aforementioned Tadhg Dall Ó hUiginn speaks tenderly of Mary too:

O Mary, daughter of *Maol Mhuire*,
until I entrusted to you my shepherding,

almost every fastness which I reached was forced,
thou lady of clinging tresses.[32]

And again:

Mary, daughter of *Maol Mhuire*,
regal in aspect, chaste in mind;
a woman excelling those of Bregia's dewy castle,
the favourite of all her kindred.[33]

The mediaeval period abounds with songs and prayers about Jesus and his mother and the passion. As a final example, the following excerpts from a mystical poem of the period may be appropriate:

Like you, O forgiving Son, may I be martyred in your martyrdom...
may I suffer thy passion with thee.

May I, in your noble life, sacrifice to you my life.
May I surrender my body in your body.
May I be poor in your poverty.

So that I be like Mary in distress,
may the seven keen shafts of sorrow
for your death pierce my heart like hers.

The thorns of his head, the spike in his footsoles,
the spear in his pap, the nail in his palms –
may these wound me, O God
tho' it be not enough to pay for your blood.

May I bear the cross beside you,
may I drink your drink of gall;
tho' to drink it were dire poison to me,
may I sit with you at one banquet.[34]

Nourishment for the strong Christo-centric and Marian devotion was derived from the sacred scriptures. The Patrician tradition of direct recourse to the scriptures remained strong after the Norman Invasion and up to the Reformation. The fourteenth century *Leabhar Breac*, is but one of many testaments to the strength and quality of that tradition:

> One of the noble gifts of the Holy Spirit is the Holy Scriptures, by which all ignorance is enlightened and all worldly afflictions comforted; by which all spiritual light is kindled and all debility is made strong. For it is through the Holy Spirit that heresy and schism are banished from the church, and all contentions and divisions reconciled. In it will well-tried counsel and appropriate instruction be found for every degree in the Church.[35]

A later writer may be forgiven for some poetic licence when he writes: 'The Old Testament and the New the Gael has in purity, and all that the inspired Prophets spoke he remembers without a mistake.'[36]

Arising from this familiarity with the scriptures, stress was laid on the concept of the Mystical Body of Christ. Personal prayer of petition was virtually always balanced off against universal need. *The Leabhar Breac,* in one of its many homilies, elaborates on the presences of Christ among his people:

> In three ways do the holy commentators understand the Body of Christ: the first Body is the humanity born from the Virgin Mary without loss to her virginity; the second Body is the holy Church, that is, the perfect assembly of all the believers whose head is the Saviour, Jesus Christ, Son of the living God; the third Body is the holy Scripture, in which is set forth the mystery of the body and blood of Christ.[37]

The Book of Psalms became the primer for aspirants to monastic life. It was their basic text for learning both literacy and spirituality. The hundred and fifty psalms were mystically divided into three fifties a term which became commonplace for designating large numbers of *anything* – warriors, saints, prayers, birds – and which determined the hundred and fifty *aves* in the Rosary.

Psalm 118 enjoyed immense prestige as a prayer to help the dead reach the fullness of life. Beginning with the Latin word *beati*, the psalm became known in Irish as *The Biait*. It was said to be 'better than every prayer... to save the soul from demons.'[38] As a prayer for the dead it was a must, as the following rather amusing tale from the fifteenth century *Book of Lismore* attests:

> Máel Póil Úa Cineatha, the abbot of the monastery of Cill Begáin, had been discussing astrology with another monk. Afterwards in his sleep he saw coming towards him a gospel-nun [i.e. apparently, a nun under the guidance of a spiritual director or soul-friend] who had died six days before. She raised a great complaint. 'How are things there woman?' said he. 'Much you care,' said she, 'discussing astrology and not saying my requiem [*echdairc*]. Woe to you,' said she. 'What requiem do you want from me, woman?' said he. 'The Biait, of course,' said she, 'the Biait after the Biait, the Biait on the Biait, the Biait beneath (or above) the Biait,' said she, all in one breath, demanding that the Biait be recited often for her. So that there is no requiem, except the Mass for the dead, that is held in greater honour by God than the Biait, as was said:
>
> > The best of wealth on earth
> > and that a man give it up for his soul's sake,
> > yet is God more grateful to him
> > for the continual recital of the Biait.[39]

Reference to purgatory is rare in this period. The term *leac na bpian* was used to describe both purgatory and hell. Both of these infernal penalty areas might be entered through a series of caves, the best known being the 'purgatory' on the island of Lough Derg.

Side by side with sound tradition and healthy faith, there were also unhealthy elements, superstitions, undue credulity in regard to miracles, and some downright abuses particularly with regard to marriage. The Irish chieftains were given to much marrying,[40] some having at least four wives.[41] The motivation varied – love, lust, land, practical politics. The Brehon Law allowed considerable latitude in marital arrangements and the

Christian church does not seem to have made Herculean efforts
to introduce any other system until the twelfth-century reform;
even then, it took a long time before the reform became effective
in this matter. While men were accused of changing their wives
as often as a modern man might change a car, the women were
often well-matched for them, one of the most notable being
Cabhlaigh Mór O'Connor who died in 1395. O'Connor was face-
tiously nicknamed *Port-na-dtrí-namhad* (which can be translated
as 'the haven of the three ships' or 'the haven of the three enemies') after a County Donegal place-name, because she had
married three warriors who were sworn enemies.[42] Nor were
these her only consorts.

Concubinage was common, not only among the laity but
among the clergy. The practice among the latter did not cause
undue scandal among lay folk, partly because of a blurring of
distinctions between cleric and layman and also because little
stigma was attached to either concubinage or illegitimacy.[43] But
even in sin, the palm must sometimes go to the cleric. One particular abbot of Abbeydorney in Kerry, for example, was widely
known to be the greatest fornicator in the region. The illegitimate offspring of the clergy frequently succeeded their fathers
to abbacies, bishoprics, canonries, and occasionally in later
times, parsonages.[44] So often were they put forward for high office in the church that in the secret consistory of October 17th
1580, when Cardinal Orsini proposed a man of illegitimate birth
for the archbishopric of Tuam, in Co Galway, Pope Gregory XIII
remarked that Irish candidates usually describe themselves as
nobles and bastards.[45]

Though taking a rather cavalier approach to sexual mores,
the Irish, both clerical and lay, took very seriously the age-old
tradition of hospitality. References to it find place in papal documents in such phrases as 'keep up hospitality which is wont,
after the custom of the country,'[46] and 'maintain hospitality according to the Irish manner.'[47] The various religious houses
were as generous in their hospitality as their resources allowed.
The abbot of St Brogan's in Co Waterford, claimed in 1477 that

he was accustomed to feed forty poor men and pilgrims at the monastery every day.[48] The tradition of monastic hospitality was well-rooted in the social tradition of the Celts, and further inspired by chapter twenty-five of St Matthew's gospel which indicates that a welcome for any guest is a welcome for Christ himself. Summing up this theme, Canice Mooney, the noted Franciscan historian, from whose writings I have drawn liberally, says:

> Hospitality, in the very widest sense of that word, flourished almost to a fault. The poor and the pilgrim, the wandering scholar, scribe, and harpist, all found welcome, food, and lodging at the many houses of hospitality that dotted the countryside. The sick poor, the lepers (in the mediaeval sense) and the orphans were all fairly adequately catered for. Despite the rigidly stratified nature of Irish society, hardly any obstacle was placed in the way of the advancement in church or society of individuals of poor or handicapped origins, provided they possessed ability and character.[49]

Penance and fasting were still strong at the end of the mediaeval period. Rising at night for the office or some other form of vigil prayer was also practised. 'At midnight,' says a foreign traveller, 'they [the Irish] rise for prayer and meditation, to which some give a full hour, others half an hour, and at the same hour they always light the fire.'[50] A quatrain from the poems of the fifteenth century poet, Tadhg Óg Ó hUiginn, shows that human weakness was always in the picture:

> I am slow to rise
> in time of matins;
> pardon me this, setting it against
> every cold night he [(St) Dominic] rose.[51]

For the purposes of meditation there was no scarcity of home or foreign reading material for those who could read Irish, Latin, English, or French. Bibles, Psalters, scripture commentaries, the *Summa* of St Thomas and other compendia of theology were

available; so too were Henry VIII's defence of the seven sacraments, St Thomas More's *Utopia*, and the same author's defence
of pilgrimage – a bestseller in Ireland no doubt! Widely read too
were devotional works such as the *Little Flowers of St Francis*,
Ludolf of Saxony's *Life of Christ*, Innocent III's *De Contemptu
Mundi*, and the most important sixteenth-century Irish publica-
tion, *Beatha Colaim Cille* (Life of St Colmcille), compiled by
Manus O'Donnell in 1532 at Port-na-dtrí-Namhad. Surviving
manuscripts from the sixteenth century also testify to firm devotion to St Michael, guardian angels, the two St Johns, and the
three women saints, Mary Magdalen, Margaret of Antioch and
Catherine of Alexandria.

At the catechetical level, 'there was an understanding that all
children should be taught by heart the Our Father, the Hail
Mary, the Creed, the Commandments, the Precepts of the
Church, and the names of the seven deadly sins. A certain number were taught to read the Psalter in Latin, and the recitation of
the penitential psalms seems to have been fairly common practice.'[52]

Summing up the pre-Reformation Irish church, Fr Canice
Mooney says:

> On the credit side there is evidence of robust faith, of high re-
> gard for the pope as vicar of Christ, of a mental outlook al-
> most inextricably interwoven with the Christian way of life,
> of great personal devotion to Christ, Our Lady and the saints,
> of friendly relations between clergy and laity. Still on the
> credit side, but not beyond criticism in all its aspects, is the
> tradition of asceticism, for instance in regard to fast and ab-
> stinence, as well as deep reverence for the relics and images
> of the saints, and the undertaking of toilsome pilgrimages.[53]

Turbulent though the centuries were in the mediaeval period,
darker clouds were gathering in the first half of the sixteenth
century as the Reformation broke over Europe and the Tudors of
England set themselves the goal of bringing Ireland to heel both
politically and religiously. As Europe divided on religious lines,

Ireland found herself among the Catholic nations and looked to
them and to the Pope himself for both temporal and spiritual
succour. An Irish bard named Costelloe, during the reign of
Elizabeth I (Tudor), apostrophised Ireland in a beautiful poem,
Róisín Dubh, which captures the spirit not only of that age but of
the centuries ahead. Here it is in the translation of James
Clarence Mangan:[54]

O my dark Rosaleen,
Do not sigh, do not weep!
The priests are on the ocean green,
They march along the deep.
There's wine... from the royal Pope,
Upon the ocean green;
And Spanish ale shall give you hope,
My Dark Rosaleen,
My own Rosaleen!
Shall glad your heart, shall give you hope,
shall give you health, and help and hope,
My Dark Rosaleen.

Over hills, and through dales,
Have I roam'd for your sake;
All yesterday I sailed with sails
On river and on lake.
The Erne... at its highest flood,
I dashed across unseen,
For there was lightning in my blood,
My Dark Rosaleen!
My own Rosaleen!
O! there was lightning in my blood,
Red lightning lightened through my blood.
My Dark Rosaleen!

All day long in unrest,
To and fro do I move.
The very soul within my breast
Is wasted for you, love!

The heart... in my bosom faints
To think of you, my Queen,
My life of life, my saint of saints,
My Dark Rosaleen!
My own Rosaleen!
To hear your sweet and sad complaints,
My life, my love, my saint of saints,
My dark Rosaleen!

Woe and pain, pain and woe,
Are my lot, night and noon,
To see your bright face clouded so,
Like to the mournful moon.
But yet... will I rear your throne
Again in golden sheen;
'Tis you shall reign, shall reign alone,
My Dark Rosaleen!
My own Rosaleen!
'Tis you shall have the golden throne,
'Tis you shall reign, and reign alone,
My Dark Rosaleen!

Over dews, over sands,
Will I fly for your weal;
Your holy delicate white hands
Shall girdle me with steel.
At home... in your emerald bowers,
From morning's dawn till e'en,
You'll pray for me, my flower of flowers,
My Dark Rosaleen!
My fond Rosaleen!
You'll think of me through daylight's hours,
My virgin flower, my flower of flowers,
My Dark Rosaleen!

I could scale the blue air,
I could plough the high hills,
Oh, I could kneel all night in prayer,

To heal your many ills!
And one... beamy smile from you
Would float like light between
My toils and me, my own, my true,
My Dark Rosaleen!
My fond Rosaleen!
Would give me life and soul anew,
A second life, a soul anew,
My Dark Rosaleen.

O! the Erne shall run red
With redundance of blood,
The earth shall rock beneath our tread,
And flames wrap hill and wood,
And gun-peal and slogan cry,
Wake many a glen serene,
Ere you shall fade, ere you shall die,
My Dark Rosaleen!
My own Rosaleen!
The Judgment Hour must first be nigh,
Ere you can fade, ere you can die,
My Dark Rosaleen!

CHAPTER 3

'Irish and Catholic'

During the sixteenth century, religion was to become the burning issue in Ireland as elsewhere in Europe. The Reformation came somewhat as a surprise in Ireland as the Irish church did not feel the pressures that seemed to be influencing the church in other countries.

Among the old Gaelic stock of the late mediaeval period there was a strong faith, though good works were not always in such abundant supply. The same may be said of the new Anglo-Norman nobility. In 1504, Gerald Fitzgerald, the Great Earl of Kildare, burned down the cathedral at Cashel. On being censured for destroying a holy place, the only excuse he offered was that he thought the archbishop was in it.[1] But the milieu in which he and his contemporaries lived was one of common faith. It was not unusual for members of the nobility to end their days in repentance within the walls of a monastery. Petitions to be clothed at death in the religious habit of the friars emerged from all strata of society. All wanted to die 'after unction and penance,'[2] while every poet worthy of the name, when the end was drawing near, sat down to write his *aithrí*, his poem of repentance. One and all shared a belief in the mercy of God rather than a dread of his anger, and believed further that the Mother of God would put in a good word on their behalf in the right place and at the right time.

Nor did the Irish have any grievance about the Bible being withheld from them; in a multitude of ways they were saturated with it: the literate could read the scriptures in the Latin *Vulgate* or *Meditationes Vitae Christi* (Meditations on the Life of Christ);

sermons and instructions were based on the scriptures, biblical poems abounded, and biblical stories and themes were told and retold as they had been from the beginning of Irish Christianity; the preaching of the friars was particularly rich in biblical lore.

As far as relations with the Pope were concerned, Canice Mooney captures the Irish attitude admirably when he says: 'Far from feeling any resentment about papal aggression, the average native Irishman of standing or education welcomed the fact that over and above the king of England stood the common father of Christendom, to whom in the last resort all could appeal for justice.'[3]

Consequently, the Irish had virtually no interest in Martin Luther or his propositions. Luther for his part never refers to Ireland, though his youth cannot have been devoid of Irish associations, since he studied law at Erfurt, an ancient Irish Benedictine foundation, about which Nicholas de Bibera wrote in his *Carmen Satiricum*,

> There are those Irishmen [in Erfurt]
> who, when high on alcohol
> proclaim that Brendan is Chief
> of the flock of the blessed,
> or that God Almighty Himself
> is Brendan's brother,
> and Brigid His Mother.
> But the ordinary man in the street
> not believing this to be true,
> judge the Irish to be
> both irreverent and daft.[4]

In Ireland, then, the Reformation was a non-event.

Not so the Reformation in England. There were already wide differences between Ireland and England in matters of language, culture and tradition. Tudor absolutism was not prepared to tolerate a further widening of the chasm between the two nations. A change of religion in England demanded similar change in Ireland. All through the sixteenth century, therefore, the Tudor monarchs pursued a relentless campaign of violence, treachery, and even diplomacy, to effect such a change.

Subverting the ancient faith in Ireland was, however, a far more formidable task than it had been among the English people, although, contrary to popular opinion, 'it is increasingly clear that for the most part they [the English] abandoned that religion with extreme reluctance.'[5] But the people of Ireland, as well as elsewhere in Europe, were frequently confused and there are many examples of outward conformity through ignorance or merely following the line of least resistance. The confusion and outward conformity was most evident in the early days under Henry VIII, but in the reign of his daughter, Elizabeth I, positions hardened. By the time of her death in 1603 it was evident that Ireland was going to remain Catholic at whatever price. The old religion, professed by the Anglo-Norman and Gaelic Irish alike, soon disclosed itself as a force making for Irish unity, and for resistance to England.[6] In Ireland the people had faith and religious zeal and were undoubtedly Catholic, but 'had not yet been roused to that passionate devotion to their religion for which they were remarkable during the next two centuries.'[7]

As early as 1539, we find complaints from one Thomas Lynch of Galway that friars 'do preach daily that every man ought, for the salvation of his soul, fight and make war against our sovereign lord the king's majesty, and if any of them die in the quarrel his soul... shall go to Heaven, as the souls of SS Peter, Paul and others, who suffer death and martyrdom for God's sake.'[8]

In August 1589, Arthur Lord Grey came to Ireland as head of the queen's forces and earned for himself a niche in history as one of Europe's and the world's most barbaric tyrants. Edmond Spencer, the Elizabethan poet, himself no angel of light, accompanied Grey on many campaigns, including the devastation of Munster. But even Spencer saw the futility of scorched-earth policies and wrote: 'Complaint was made against him [Grey], that he was a bloodie man, and regarded not the life of her subjects no more than dogges, but had wasted and consumed all, so as now she had nothing almost left, but to raigne in their ashes.'[9] The war continued until both the Old Gaelic and Anglo-Norman nobility were brought to their knees. The battle of Kinsale in 1601 delivered the *coup-de-grace* to the old Irish world.

Among the numerous victims of the Tudor reign of terror were Archbishop Creagh of Armagh who died in the Tower of London, Archbishop O'Hurley of Cashel who was savagely tortured before being hanged in Dublin, and Dr Nicholas Saunders, the papal legate during the Desmond Wars, who, after many hair-breadth escapes, eventually fell victim to starvation; 'his body afterwards found in a roadside hovel, mangled since death by the attacks of wild beasts, whose ordinary ferocity was rendered desperate by the general destruction of the usual production of nature.'[10]

As the idea of nationality evolved in Europe, and as church and state there tended to find their separate levels, in Ireland the elements of nationality and catholicity tended to blend; in fact, they became virtually synonymous. In the journal of the Protestant Dean of Cork for the year 1691 we find the term *English gentleman* used to include Irish Protestants; Francis Rogers a few years later remarks that the Protestants 'are not pleased to be called Irish at home.'[11]

It is a curious thing that the Catholic community in England, who in the seventeenth century were a severely persecuted minority, were never well-disposed towards Ireland or its suffering people. Count D'Avaux, writing to Louis XIV in April 1689, commented that 'The Irish also recognise that the English who are close to the king, even the Catholics, are their greatest enemies.'[12] A letter of Bishop O'Moloney's, which Archbishop King thought worth quoting, supports this view. He says: 'Nor is there any Englishman, Catholic or other, of what quality or degree soever alive will stick to sacrifice all Ireland for to save the least interest of his own in England; and would as willingly see all Ireland over inhabited by English of whatsoever religion, as by the Irish.'[13]

In the first half of the seventeenth century, prior to the

Cromwellian blight, the church had some breathing space in which the hierarchy was strengthened and religious orders, especially the Franciscans, expanded. Many young men went to the Continent where they received education for the priesthood in one of the newly-founded Irish Colleges. This link with the Continent was a real lifeline for the faith in Ireland during the darker days ahead.

In 1625, after almost a century of effort to subvert the Catholic faith in Ireland, one John Roche from New Ross gives a Protestant assessment of the situation: 'the very ground the Irish tread, the air they breathe, the climate they share, the very sky above them, all seem to draw them to the religion of Rome, so much so that if one of them appears to abandon it the very enemies of the Catholic faith doubt his sincerity.'[14]

Under Queen Elizabeth I's successor, James I of England (VI of Scotland), a systematic plantation of Ulster was planned and executed. It was not the first plantation (the Tudors had planted large tracts of Munster and Leinster) but it was the most successful. The English government confiscated the counties of Donegal, Derry, Fermanagh, Tyrone, Armagh and Cavan, and granted the lands to Protestants from England and Scotland who were prepared to accept the King of England as head of the church in Ireland. Settlers from London were granted large tracts of land in County Derry and proceeded to fortify the city of Colm Cille and change its name to Londonderry. The plantation caused massive upheaval and a deep resentment took root among the dispossessed Irish, not only because they had lost their land but also because they 'suffered from the bitter, intolerant spirit of the new settlers, who were mostly Puritans.'[15] This resentment flared up into a bloody massacre of the new Settlers in 1641. The number said to have been killed in this uprising was wildly exaggerated in England, and, ever since the 'massacre of '41', the colonists have not trusted Catholics. 'When Oliver Cromwell landed at Dublin with a puritan army in 1649,' says Aidan Clarke, 'his mission was not only conquest, but also revenge. The indiscriminate inhumanity with which that revenge was exacted... became indelibly impressed upon the folk memory of the Irish.'[16]

Cromwell is seen in Ireland as the arch-destroyer, but the attempt to wipe out Catholicism as well as the culture which sustained it had been in progress long before him. Of this on-going campaign to obliterate every vestige of Irish civilisation, Alice Curtayne writes:

A feature of the war waged upon the Irish in the seventeenth century strangely recalled an aspect of the Viking invasions: the destruction of the books and manuscripts. The policy now was to destroy the Gaelic tradition, embodied in this literature. The books were marked down to be got rid of. Bishop Lynch in *Cambrensis Eversus*, published in 1622 says: 'Certain it is that within the memory of our fathers the English burned with savage rage for the destruction of our Irish documents.' He goes on to describe how, in the time of Elizabeth, the English soldiers rifled the houses of citizens and made a special search for manuscripts. In the town garrisons, the soldiers dismembered the old vellum books, handing out leaves to school-boys and telling them to make covers for their copy-books out of them. Numbers of the pages were seen in tailors' rooms, cut into clothes patterns. No one will ever be able to assess the quantity of books and manuscripts that were burned. In his *Analecta*, Bishop Rothe tells us: 'If any officers of the Government heard of a fragment of manuscript history being in the possession of a private individual, it was at once begged or bought, or, if neither money nor entreaty were strong enough, threats and commands immediately followed.' The love of the Irish for these pathetic treasures and their sorrow, which they could not conceal, when they were wrested from them and destroyed, made the Government all the more determined in its campaign against them.[17]

In his onslaught on the Catholic religion Cromwell struck right at the heart of the matter by viciously attacking the Mass, so that when a town was captured, the clergy were almost invariably excluded from pardon.[18] 'I meddle not with any man's conscience,' he wrote on October 19th 1649 when demanding the surrender of New Ross, 'but if by liberty of conscience you mean a liberty to exercise the Mass, I judge it best to use plain dealing, and let you know where the parliament of England have power, that will not be allowed of.'[19] Bishop Lynch, in his *Cambrensis Eversus* elaborates on the doleful aftermath:

> Under the Protectorate it was death to harbour or protect a priest; death not to disclose their hiding-places 'in the caverns of the mountains, the chasms of the quarry, and in the dark recesses of the forest.' And 'any person accidentally meeting and recognising a priest was subject to have his ears cut off, and to be flogged naked through the town, if he did not inform.' 'Many times,' says Bruodin, 'were these iniquitous laws enforced in Ireland.'[20]

The most notorious events of the reign of terror during Cromwell's short stay in Ireland were the massacres in Drogheda and Wexford. Of the Wexford massacre, the exiled Catholic bishop of the area later wrote from Antwerp:

> On one day I lost for the cause of God and the faith, all that I possessed: it was 11th October 1649. On that most lamentable day my native city of Wexford, abounding in wealth, ships, and merchandise, was destroyed by the sword, and given a prey to the infuriated soldiers, by Cromwell, that English pest of hell. There before God's altar fell many sacred victims, priests of the Lord; others, who were seized outside the precincts of the church, were scourged with whips; others were hanged; some were arrested and bound with chains; and others were put to death by various most cruel tortures. The best blood of the citizens was shed; the very squares were inundated with it, and there was scarcely a house that was not defiled with carnage and full of wailing.[21]

To pay off the soldiers and those who had otherwise invested in

the Cromwellian campaign in Ireland, nine counties were confiscated. Not satisfied with that plunder, the Cromwellians de-
vised a further plan, namely, to gettoise the Irish population and
consign them to the west of the Shannon, thus reserving the re-
mainder of the country for Protestant planters. The infamous
phrase 'To hell or to Connacht,' attributed to Cromwell, effectively called for the extermination of all Catholics or their ban-
ishment west of the Shannon to Clare and Connacht, the least
fertile and productive part of Ireland.

The Cromwellian interpretation of the term Irish was a novel
one and took the 'Old English' by surprise. These 'Old English'
were a large and influential group of Anglo-Norman aristocracy
who looked on themselves as anything but Irish. They belonged
to the towns and lived in a state of more or less perpetual hostility towards the inhabitants of the rural hinterlands. Politically,
they were nearly always loyal to the king of England but despite
their political loyalty they also remained intensely loyal to their
Catholic faith. (Carrickfergus was the only town in the whole
country to go over officially to Protestantism.) Suddenly these
Catholic loyalist townspeople found themselves disenfran-
chised and forced to make common cause with their Gaelic Irish
co-religionists and erstwhile enemies. It is, then, an ironic fact
that 'the union of Catholics in Ireland was, from first to last, a
Protestant achievement, not a Catholic one.'[22] In later times,
when a person was identified as 'Irish,' there was an automatic
assumption that they were also 'Catholic'. This, too, was a
Protestant achievement.

The Cromwellian Settlement, as it came to be called, was the
beginning of landlordism in Ireland – a scourge that was to last
until the turn of the twentieth century. Like the earlier settlers in
the northern counties, the Cromwellian planters were also bitterly sectarian and philistine.

With the triumph of Cromwell and the Puritans in the mid-
seventeenth century, France again became a haven. In 1652,
through Cardinal Mazarin's diplomacy, 20,000 men of the
Catholic army in Ireland were transferred to the army of France.

A considerable number of proscribed priests also settled in France, especially in Paris. Fr Vincent de Paul, later saint, extended his kindly hand to aid them in their hardship. Some became *curés*, while others crowded into the schools and universities where their talent and scholarship were recognised and rewarded. The office of Procurator of the German Nation of the University of Paris was practically the monopoly of Irishmen from beginning to end of the seventeenth century. The 'German Nation' here meant students and scholars from northern and north-eastern Europe.[23]

The French king did his part for the exiles, as the recreant Lord O'Brien, himself an Irishman, testifies: 'All the youth of that kingdom [Ireland] are sent over into France where they are bred up to the Church, Law or Sword... the French king keeps above 2,000 always in colleges for divinity and law and has now for the most part in his service all those whose estates were forfeited.'[24] Such information from O'Brien was sad reading indeed for the English government to whom it was sent, as England was now feeling the effects of the Irish Brigade, already becoming legendary for its spirit and reckless bravery. The king of France, on the other hand, must have felt generously repaid for patronage bestowed on these exiles: in approximately half a century (1700-1750), two hundred thousand Irishmen gave their lives on Continental battlefields, chiefly in the service of France.

Though failing to destroy Catholicism, the Elizabethans and Cromwellians did succeed in establishing a permanent Protestant ascendancy of those planters whom the Munster poet, Ó Bruadair, styles, 'rogues formed from the dregs of each base trade, who range themselves snugly in the houses of the noblest chiefs, as proud and genteel as if sons of gentlemen.'[25] Lecky, the noted and unusually perceptive historian of the times, does not see a mere amorphous mob of squalid, ignorant 'papists' in their mud cabins – a level beyond which many of his contemporaries and countrymen did not see. Instead he had glimpses of that other Ireland in which 'ejected proprietors whose name might be traced in the Annals of the Four Masters, or around the sculptured crosses of Clonmacnoise, might be found in abject poverty hanging around the land that had lately been their own, shrinking from servile labour as from an intolerable pollution and still receiving a secret homage from their old tenants.'[26]

When the Catholic Stuart King James II ascended to the throne in England in 1685, he had the goodwill and support of Irish Catholics. In 1689 he called an Irish parliament (*the Patriot Parliament*). It was mainly a gathering of Catholics and 'produced legislation that was a landmark of religious toleration in an environment hostile to it.'[27] Among other things it passed an Act of Liberty of Conscience which 'guaranteed religious freedom, allowed the Church of Ireland to retain its property, but insisted that all were to pay tithe for the support of the clergy of their own denomination.'[28]

During the Jacobite Wars (1688-91) Irish Catholics supported James II in his struggle to retain the monarchy against the advance of the Protestant party led by his son-in-law, William of Orange. William, with the backing of the Protestant ascendancy and the help of English, Dutch, Irish, Danish, and French-Huguenot mercenaries, carried the day at the Boyne and Aughrim, and the war in Ireland ended with the Treaty of Limerick.

William was too weak to stand by his word, and the Treaty of Limerick, an honourable settlement signed in 1691, was broken almost immediately. During the half century that followed, the members of the Protestant ascendancy parliament in Dublin busily engaged themselves in enacting a Penal Code against the Irish people who were already almost crushed out of existence. From now on there was officially no such being as an Irish Catholic: the legal term was the pejorative *papist*. John Bowes, chief baron of the exchequer summed up the situation in 1759 when he declared that the law did not presume an Irish Catholic to exist except for the purposes of punishment.[29] No Catholic was allowed to teach or to get education in or out of the country. Transgressors forfeited their property, and were declared ineligible to become legal guardians or the executors or beneficiaries

of wills. Catholics were not allowed to bear arms and magis-
trates were free to break into their houses in search of such
weapons. Gunsmiths could not take Catholic apprentices.
Catholics were forbidden to harbour or support a priest, or to
bury their dead in the graveyards of suppressed monasteries. It
was proposed in parliament, but not legislated, that every priest
found in Ireland after 1 May 1720, should have the letter 'P'
branded on the cheek with a red-hot iron. On the other hand, a
handsome annuity was offered to any priest willing to adopt the
Protestant faith – takers were few. Anyone permitting Mass to be
celebrated in their home was subject to a heavy fine and a year in
jail. In 1733, marriages celebrated by priests or friars were declared null. Mixed marriages between Catholics and Protestants
were forbidden by the civil law. If a Protestant man married a
Catholic he fell under the full weight of the Penal Laws. If a
Protestant woman married a Catholic she was disinherited.[30]

Greed and privilege rather than religion were at the root of
much of the persecution of Catholics. Because the primary motive was material gain, the ascendancy class had no real desire to
convert the papists, for their ambition was to corner as much
wealth as possible among the smallest number of people. Lecky
puts it in a sentence: 'It was intended to make them [the Irish
Catholics] poor and to keep them poor, to crush them in every
germ of enterprise, to degrade them into a servile caste who
could never hope to rise to the level of their oppressor.'[31] No
wonder that MacLysaght could bluntly state in his *Irish Life in
the Seventeenth Century*:

> The penal laws enacted against Irish Catholics in the eigh-
> teenth century may be regarded as the worst in the annals of
> religious intolerance, not only because they were devised at a
> date when the world had freed itself from mediaeval ideas,
> but also because in themselves they were infamous, relying
> as they did on treachery and dishonour for their execution
> and being imposed on the majority by a minority, powerful
> only by reason of external backing.[32]

Here was the rub. The persecution of Protestants in France and Spain was cited to justify the savage laws now passed against Irish Catholics, but in those countries the members of the persecuted sect formed a small minority, while Ireland was unique in that the persecuted formed the vast majority of the population. The persecuting minority relied on the military force of England to operate the barbarous system.

Legal inducements offered to Catholics to change their religion were based, not on spiritual values, but on personal ambition to climb the social ladder or retain, at least in part, hereditary estates. Yet converts from Gaelic stock were few, and fewer still those who made the religious transition with a clear conscience. The case of the Irish poet, Piaras Mac Gearailt (1700-1791) is typical of the uneasy conscience:

> 'Tis sad for me to cleave to Calvin or perverse Luther, but the weeping of my children, the spoiling them of flocks and land brought streaming floods from my eyes and descent of tears... There is a part of the Saxon Lutheran religion which, though not from choice, I have accepted that I do not like – that never a petition is addressed to Mary, the mother of Christ, nor honour nor privilege nor prayer, and yet it is my opinion that it is Mary who is... tree of light and crystal of Christianity, the glow and precious lantern of the sky, the sunny chamber in the house of glory, flood of graces and Cliona's wave of mercy.[33]

The poverty of the people at the time of the Treaty of Limerick is scarcely imaginable. The economic conditions of the Catholic people were probably the lowest ever reached in Western Europe. Dean Swift, himself part of the ascendancy class, spoke of 'the miserable dress and diet and dwelling of the people... The families of farmers who pay great rents living in filth and nastiness upon buttermilk and potatoes, not a shoe or stocking to their feet, or a house so convenient as an English hog-sty to receive them.'[34] Of the 184,000 houses recorded for tax purposes in the country, 160,000 of them had no chimney.[35]

Like the colonisation process, the persecution and the application of the penal laws did not always operate evenly or universally. There were failures and half-hearted efforts, due to the sheer inability of governments to carry through their policies. Occasionally, there was to be found a humane member of the ascendancy ready to bend or ignore the unjust laws.

Of all the centuries of Irish history, the eighteenth was surely the saddest. Stripped of every vestige of human dignity which the destroyer was capable of removing, the people were ground into the dust. But as the trampling of the grape produces the wine, so the grinding of the common people brought to the surface the riches and inner resources of their faith. The result was a wonderful blossoming of popular piety in the form of folk-prayers which fed the spiritual life of the people. These prayers, together with the rosary and the occasional Mass celebrated at the risk of one's life and only in the remotest of places, gave strength to an already religious people.

The effect of the penal laws on the Irish led to a strengthening of the faith, a deepening of conviction, a revealing, through suffering and deprivation, of the real value the people placed on their religion and particularly on the Mass. Under the pressure of the penal laws, the links between 'Irish' and 'Catholic' grew stronger for, stripped of political power and ownership of the land, Catholics, whether native or 'Old English,' came to see that their common faith gave them an identity which no persecutor could take from them.

After his visit to Ireland, John Wesley gave his assessment of the Irish situation:

At least ninety-nine in a hundred of the native Irish remained in the religion of their forefathers. The Protestants whether in Dublin or elsewhere are almost all transplanted from England. Nor is it any wonder that those who are born Papists generally live and die such, when the Protestants can find no better way to convert them than penal laws and acts of parliament.[36]

The transplanting from England of which John Wesley spoke went on at a considerable pace and repeated efforts were made when schemes failed. The extent of it may be gauged from the following table:[37]

In 1530 Catholics owned 100% of the land.
In 1641 Catholics owned 59% of the land.
In 1703 Catholics owned 14% of the land.
In 1778 Catholics owned 5% of the land.

In 1974 Fr Diarmuid Ó Laoghaire published a collection of five hundred and thirty-nine folk-prayers. It is not an exhaustive collection, nor is it the only collection, but it is indicative of the riches of the popular piety that so many have survived. Neither the authorship nor the date of composition is known in most cases, but the seventeenth and eighteenth centuries can lay claim to many of them. A glance at the contents page of Fr Ó Laoghaire's book indicates their wide range: prayers when rising in the morning, to one's guardian angel (so familiar in the Gaelic world that when saluting a person the plural form is used, i.e. to include the guardian angel); prayers of blessing and thanksgiving before and after meals; prayers before work, before a journey, before death; prayers associated with repentance, with the rosary of Mary, with the passion of Christ, with the Holy Spirit, the Eternal Father and the Trinity; prayers to Christ in his glory and to the saints, as well as a host of others; but the longest list of all is the collection of close on a hundred beautiful prayers concerning the Mass.[38]

In *Our Mass our Life*, another of Fr Ó Laoghaire's publications, there are some fine examples of prayers relating to the Mass. It is difficult to make a choice due to the beauty of each. In the original Irish these prayers are, for the most part, in verse. Here is a prayer to be recited on the way to Mass. It comes from the Kerry tradition and reflects a sense of the Communion of Saints: 'We walk together with the Virgin Mary and the other holy people who accompanied her only Son on the Hill of Calvary.'[39] Another beautiful prayer to the 'King of the blessed

Sunday' is my next example. The term 'King of the blessed Sunday' is a warm and familiar title in Gaelic, corresponding to the scriptural *Kurios* (the risen Lord). This prayer was associated with a special *coróin* or rosary:

> *Céad fáilte romhat, a Rí an Domhnaigh bheannaithe*
> *do tháinig le cabhar chughainn tar éis na seachtaine.*
> *Corraigh mo chos go moch chun Aifrinn,*
> *corraigh im bhéal na briathra beannaithe,*
> *corraigh mo chroí agus díbir an ghangaid as.*
> *Féachaim suas ar Mhac na Banaltran,*
> *agus ar a haon-Mhac trócaireach,*
> *mar is é is fearr a cheannaigh sinn*
> *agus gur leis féin beo is marbh sinn.*

> (A hundred welcomes to you, O King of the Blessed Sunday
> who has come to help us after the week.
> My feet guide early to Mass,
> part my lips with blessed words,
> stir up my heart and banish out of it all spite.
> I look up to the Son of the Nurse,
> her one and only Son of Mercy,
> for He it is who has so excellently redeemed us
> and His we are whether we live or die).[40]

That prayer was said on the large beads of the rosary and the following on the small beads:

> V. A hundred welcomes to you, O King of glorious Sunday.
> O Son of the Virgin and King of Glory,
> R. O sweet Jesus, O son of Mary,
> have mercy on us.[41]

Then on sight of the church or entering it:

> Blessed is the House of God
> and I myself greet Him
> where He is with the twelve apostles.
> May the Son of God bless us.

Blessed are you, O holy Father,
Blessed are you, O Temple of the Holy Spirit,
Blessed are you, O Church of the Trinity.[42]

Further greetings, to the altar, and to the cross and the crucified,
are set in another versified prayer:

Hail to you, O altar,
O beautiful, flowering, green cross,
let not my soul pass you by.
May you keep me in the state of grace,
may you convert us to the right way,
may you enlarge our hearts to be filled with glory,
may you fill our eyes with tears of repentance,
may you give us our share of every Mass
that is celebrated in Rome today
and throughout the whole world. Amen.[43]

Reference to Christ as the 'poor crucified rider' is well established in Irish prayers, the notion of Christ riding the cross being
a familiar image in high-class Irish poetry of several centuries
prior to the days of persecution. Other features of these prayers
are references to the universal church, and above all to Rome.
The Mother of God is frequently mentioned and many prayers
are in the plural because of a keen awareness of the community
of God's people, the Body of Christ.

And here's a quatrain summing up the Irish peoples' notion
of their ideal priest:

B'áil liom sagart breá sultarach pléisiurtha,
lán de chreideamh is carthanach nádúrtha,
a bheadh béideach le bochtaibh is cneasta lena thréadaí,
ach níorbh áil liom stolluire fé chulaith mhín an Aon-Mhic.

(I would like a fine, pleasant, cheerful priest,
full of faith, charitable and kindly,
who would have sympathy for the poor and be gentle with
his flock,

but I would not like a good-for-nothing in the fair livery of
the Only Son).[44]

Fr Ó Laoghaire compares this peasant verse with the ideal proposed in the Second Vatican Council's *Decree on the Ministry and
Life of Priests*: 'priests will find great help in the possession of
those virtues which are deservedly esteemed in human affairs,
such as goodness of heart, sincerity, strength and constancy of
character, civility...'[45]

For every part of the Mass the people had not one but several
beautiful prayers. In such a work as this I can do little more than
refer my readers to the sources.[46]

However, I cannot refrain from quoting a little more. The following is a translation of a 'welcoming prayer' after the
Consecration of the Mass:

A hundred thousand welcomes to You, Body of the Lord,
You, son of her the Virgin, the brightest, most adorned,
Your death in such fashion
On the tree of the passion
Has saved Eve's race and put sin to death.

I am a poor sinner to You appealing,
Reward me not as my sins may be;
O Jesus Christ I deserve Your anger,
But turn again and show grace to me.

Jesus who bought us,
Jesus who taught us,
Jesus of the united prayer [i.e. the rosary],
Do not forget us
Now nor in the hour of death.

O crucified Jesus, do not leave us,
You poured Your blood for us, O forgive us,
May the Grace of the Spirit for ever be with us,
And whatever we ask may the Son of God give us.[47]

The joy and the welcome at the Consecration of the Mass was

phenomenal. Even into the twentieth century the remoter and more thoroughly Gaelic areas reflected a certain after-glow of the genuine Gaelic piety. Eilís Ní Chorra describes a Mass she attended in Achill, Co Mayo, early in the century:

> The church was packed and never before (or since) have I seen and heard such fervour. The congregation attended Mass in every sense of the word, making the responses aloud with the altar boys, and at the Consecration there was such a cry of welcome to our Lord in the Blessed Sacrament – Céad míle fáilte, a Thiarna (a hundred thousand welcomes Lord) – that the tears came to my eyes – and I am not an emotional person.[48]

To Eoghan Ruadh Ó Súilleabháin, the eighteenth-century poet and darling lyricist of Munster, is attributed a beautiful version of the Our Father:

Ár nAthair atá ar Neamh
do cheap sinn féin ar dtúis,
go naomhaíthear t'ainm
is go dtagaimid go léir id dhún,
t'aon-toil bheannaithe
ar an dtalamh go ndéanam súd
fé mar dheineann gach neach ar Neamh
nuair a théid id dhún.
An t-arán geal do cheapais féin dúinn tabhair
is ár gcionta ar fad go maithir féinig dúinn,
fé mar a mhaith an Mac don fhear gan néall 'na shúil,
Ná lig sinn sa ríocht san as nach féidir teacht,
in aon drochní ná i dtintibh daora i dteas,
ach, amen, a Chríost, agus lig sinn go léir isteach.

(Our Father who art in Heaven
who fashioned us in the beginning,
may your name be made holy
and may we all enter your house,
your holy and only will

may we do it on earth
as does everyone in Heaven who enters in.
Give the bright bread you made for us,
and all our sins may you yourself forgive
as the Son forgave the man of the sightless eyes.
Do not let us enter the kingdom of the dead
in a state of sin, nor into the heat of hell's fires,
but amen, O Christ, do you admit us all).[49]

There was a custom, still practised by older people, of taking a drink – or three sips – of water after Holy Communion. Here is an accompanying prayer from Mayo and Kerry:

Sláinte an Árd-Mhic do leath a ghéaga
ar chrann na Páise chun sinn a shaoradh
agus sláinte na mná mánla do rug a Mac gan chéile
agus sláinte Naomh Pádraig do bheannaigh Éire.

(Health to the noble Son who spread his arms
on the tree of the passion to free us,
and health to the gentle woman who without man gave birth
to her son,
and health to St Patrick who blessed Ireland).[50]

Fidelity to the Mass was the aspect of the faith which outshone all other expressions of it in the penal times. The seventeenth and eighteenth centuries were noted as the age of the Mass-rock. It was also the age of the *Sagart Aroon* (the darling priest), as the people affectionately designated their pastor: by night he ministered to them, and in the remote caves and bogs, in the shelter of a hedge, in a shack or beside a fence or on a boulder or rock, he would celebrate the outlawed Mass. Secret signs, passed from one to another across the countryside, would signal the time of sacrifice, so that those who could not risk being present could join in spirit at the exact time of celebration.

Though I am unable to recall the source, I once read of a John Mezzafalce, a missionary returning from China on an English ship. In the first decade of the eighteenth century he found himself weather-bound for months in Galway. Giving his testimony as an eyewitness in a letter to the Pope, he spoke of the,

> constancy and devotedness with which they [the Irish] adhered to the Holy See... though they were ridiculed and laughed at yet they all faithfully observed the fast and abstinence... In order to hear Mass on Sundays and holy days, the men and women go out from the city, for Mass is not permitted within the city walls... This constancy amid so many persecutions is quite general and shared by almost all of every condition and sex and age...'

But this was also the age of the priest-hunters, the most infamous being perhaps John Garzia, an Iberian Jew, and Edward Tyrrell, a renegade Catholic who was executed in 1713 for bigamy. In a surviving manuscript of Dr Nicholas Madgett, Bishop of Kerry from 1753 to 1774, we learn that the following scale of reward obtained for the priest-hunters of those days:

£30.00 sterling or current money for a simple priest;
£50.00 for a bishop;
£40.00 for a vicar-general;
£50.00 for a Jesuit.[51]

The loathing of the people for the priest-hunter is typified in a quatrain by Tadhg Ó Neachtain, on the occasion of seeing the body of Tyrrell hanging on the gibbet:

Maith do thoradh, a chrainn!
Rath do thoraidh ar gach aon craoibh:
Truagh gan crainnte Inse Fáil
Lán ded' thoradh gach aon lá!

(Good is thy fruit O tree!
The luck of thy fruit on every bough;
Would that all the trees of Ireland
Were full of thy fruit every single day!)[52]

While there were exceptions, the behaviour of the clergy during the persecution was admirable. 'We shall not abandon our flocks,' wrote St Oliver Plunkett, primate and martyr, 'till we are compelled by force to do so: we will first suffer imprisonment and other torments. We have already suffered so much on the mountains, in huts and caverns, and we have acquired such a habit that for the future suffering will be less severe and troublesome.'[53] John Brennan, Bishop of Waterford and Lismore, writing in June 1672, says that 'In the whole territory of the Diocese of Lismore which I have visited it is incredible how delighted the poor Catholics were, no bishop having been seen in many parts of the diocese for the past forty years. There was not a day but I had to give Confirmation at least twice, and my Vicar-General, who accompanied me, stated that fifteen thousand persons were confirmed, some of them being sixty years of age.[54] A few months later, in his report to Rome, he says: 'the people generally speaking are very religious and pious, leading a Christian life without great fault or many scandals. They hold tenaciously (*tenacissimi*) to the Catholic faith and have great reverence for the Apostolic See.'[55] The closeness between clergy and people was always there but in the days of common misfortune, it grew stronger as the people who had lost all saw that the priest was willing to share their plight and minister to them in their misery. John Banim (1798-1842) captures the spirit:

> Who in the winter night, Sagart Aroon,
> When the cold blast did bite, Sagart Aroon,
> Came to my cabin door,
> And on the earthen floor,
> Knelt by me, sick and poor,
> Sagart Aroon.

The oppressed Irish did not rely wholly on bended knees for survival. The *Bon Dieu* had given them a sharp, quick and often devastating wit, and whether or not he meant it to be thus used, the Irish often employ this gift for purposes of immersing the opposition in oceans of withering satire. One of the most celebrated quatrains of the period sets out a comparison between the foundation-stone of the Catholic Church and that of the

Anglican Communion. It was collected in the West of Ireland by
by Douglas Hyde, himself a Protestant:

> Ná trácht ar an mhinistéir gallda
> Ná ar a chreideamh gan beann, gan bhrí,
> Mar níl mar bhuan-chloch dá theampuill,
> Ach magairlí Aonraoí Rí.

Literally,

> Don't mention the minister foreign,
> Without rhyme or reason his faith,
> And his church has no stone of foundation
> But the stones of Henry the Eight.

At the catechetical level, *Parrthas an Anama* (Paradise of the Soul)
was published by the Franciscan, Anton Gearnon, in 1645 and
was widely used for generations afterwards. An idea of its tone
and content may be gleaned from the following excerpt from
chapter eight:

Q. What should the Christian do at midnight?

A. He should perform matins and say the canonical hours or
the Hours of Mary or the Crown of Jesus or the Rosary or the
Litanies of Jesus, Mary or the saints or any prayer for the
souls in purgatory; in addition he should spend some time
thinking on the Passion of Christ, on his last end and on the
souls in hell and in purgatory who sleep not, but are being
burned in unquenchable fires. Let him consider likewise that
the angels and saints in heaven are not sleeping, but are for
ever praising God, and let him imitate them especially at that
time; for there is no better time for prayer than that, since the
mind is then quiet and at rest and free from worldly care and
trouble.

Q. Is there any other reason besides that for making these
prayers at midnight rather than at any other time?

A. Yes: firstly, because at that hour Christ was born and also,
according to some of the holy fathers, will come to judgment.
As well as that, in the Old Testament it was customary to
pray at that time, whence the Psalmist and King, David, says

that although many things demanded his attention: *Media nocte surgebam ad confitendum tibi* [Ps 118 – I rise at midnight to give praise to thee]. Christ our Lord taught the same thing in the New Testament, as we find in St Luke the Evangelist in the 6th c. *Erat Jesus pernoctans in oratione Dei*, i.e. Jesus spent the night in prayer; and most of the saints of the Church imitated Him in this matter. This fine custom is still kept up as a rule by the Religious Orders and by other holy people. It is not long since the same holy practice was common throughout Ireland among all sorts of people who loved God and had a care for the health of their souls.[56]

Side by side with the occasional Mass and instruction and the handing on of a living faith from parents to their children, people derived spiritual nourishment from a succession of religious exercises – pilgrimages, patterns, fasts, and and many other age-old practices.

Pilgrims returning from Lough Derg in Penal Times brought home crosses (penal crosses) inscribed with the date of their visit. Despite the legal prohibition, the pilgrimage and pattern (i.e. patron's festival) refused to die. They were too deeply rooted in the cultural background of the people and a need in their otherwise bleak lives. In 1609 Sir Arthur Chichester complained to the privy council that Jesuits and priests from abroad flocked to Inishgaltaghe (Inish Cealtra in Lough Derg on the lower Shannon) 'to give absolution and pardons, and they come and go hence with the swallows... making a yearly revenue of poor and rich.'[57] This particular centre for pilgrimage came to an end as a religious gathering-place of note in 1839, because, as Professor O'Donovan notes, 'some ill-behaved young rascals' took to the habit of carrying off young girls by force from the crowd thus providing themselves with 'fresh consorts for the ensuing year.'[58]

Fasting, even in those 'bad old days,' was not neglected, and Dr Madgett in his *Constitutio Ecclesiastica* wonders about the official church fasts and the popular notion of fast: 'What is to be thought,' he poses, 'of the old way of fasting among our country people, what they call "black fast" (*dobh Carise*) i.e. they take two full meals without meat, eggs or any kind of milk-meats, only bread, water and pottage or very rarely ale?'[59]

The passion of Christ, too, is a constant companion and it must have provided consolation for the people in their own hour of trial. Here is one popular prayer on the subject:

> O Lord, You were tortured on Friday,
> And were crucified on the cross of pain,
> You were tightly bound with chords,
> And were given to drink
> A draught of bitter-tasting gall.
> But, thanks to God, Your persecutors failed;
> You saved the countless thousands
> Whom the fiends held in bondage,
> And to whom day was as night
> Until they went to the brightness of Paradise
> Where they found sweet music and delights,
> And a mantle white with which to clothe the King and His host. Amen.[60]

A prayer appropriate to bed-time, or perhaps to be recited in bed with one's arms folded in the form of a cross, runs:

> *A Rí an Aoine*
> *Do shín do ghéuga ar an gcroich*
> *A Thighearna ar ar fhulaing tú*
> *Na mílte agus na céudta lot*
> *Sínimid síos*
> *Faoi dhídhean do sgéithe anocht*
> *Agus go sgapaidh tú orainn toradh an chroinn*
> *Ar céusadh air do chorp. Amen.*[61]

> (O King of the Friday,
> Whose limbs on the cross were bound;
> O Lord, Who suffered
> Sharp pain in many a wound,
> We lay down to rest
> Beneath the shield of Your might;

May fruit from the tree of Your Passion
Fall on us this night. Amen).[62]

And yet another prayer brings out the warmth and concern for
those members of the Body of Christ who have passed into the
other world. In translation from the Irish it runs:

We offer up a *Pater* and an *Ave* in honour of God and the
Virgin Mary
for the poor souls who are suffering the pain of purgatory,
and especially for the souls of our own relations;
for every poor soul for whom there is none to pray;
for every soul in great and urgent need;
for the soul that has last departed from this world,
and for every poor soul burdened with the guilt of an imper-
fect confession,
a forgotten Mass, or a penance not performed.
We include them all in this prayer:
may God release them tonight. Amen.[63]

I do not know the date of composition of that prayer but it may
be of nineteenth-century origin. The sentiments expressed are
most familiar to me from childhood. It may well be a prayer
forming part of 'the trimmings of the rosary' – that litany of
prayers for a variety of intentions which was part of the prayer-
life of virtually every household in the country. Note also its
construction, a sort of *lorica*, in its naming of the different categories and needs and intentions.

With the passage of time the intensity of the persecution gave
way to a sort of acknowledgement of the *status quo* in relation to
the 'conversion' of Ireland. Many influential Protestants closed
their eyes to what was happening in relation to Catholic worship. All over the land there sprang up little *Mass-houses*, in
town and country alike, and to these hovels the people would
resort.

Finally, the element of fun and humour was never far from
the Irish even in times of persecution, and this no less in their reli-

gious practice than in any other aspect of their lives. I find the
following anecdote of particular interest. In his memoirs, Arthur
O'Neill, the blind musician, recounts an incident relating to
Christmas 1750 or thereabouts. Arriving at Navan, Co Meath, he
met one Thady Elliot, a fellow harpist who might be described
as the resident musician at the little chapel of the Catholic community. O'Neill himself takes up the story:

> On a Christmas Day, Thady was to play at the Roman
> Catholic chapel of Navan, and a humorous fellow in Navan
> took Thady to a public house and promised to give him a gal-
> lon of whiskey if he rattled up *Planxty Connor* at the time of
> the Elevation, which Thady promised to do. Accordingly
> when Mass commenced on Christmas morning Thady as
> usual played some sacred airs until the elevation, and for the
> sake of the whiskey and to be as good as his word he lilted up
> Planxty Connor. The priest, who was a good judge of music,
> knew the tune but at that solemn stage of the ceremony he
> could not speak to Thady. But to show his disapprobation he
> stamped violently on the altar – so much so that the people
> exclaimed in Irish, 'Dar Dhia, tá an sagart a' damhsa!' that is,
> 'By God, the priest is dancing!' However, after playing
> *Planxty* for some short time he resumed his usual tunes. But
> when Mass was over Thady was severely reproved and dis-
> missed.[64]

What intrigues me about the story is not the humour, nor the
summary dismissal, nor the playing of *Planxty Connor* at the
Elevation – which may be Thady Elliot's only claim to immortal
memory – but the attitude of the worshippers. They seem to
have accepted the notion that the priest's most appropriate response to the dance-music – even in the circumstances – was to
dance. It seemed right, and is therefore a fine illustration of that
Celtic trait pointed out by Alexander Carmichael, that they were
'unable to see and careless to know where the secular began and
the religious ended.'[65]

The really important fact about the age of persecution is that

the faith survived. There was little in the way of development,
except for the blossoming of popular prayers and the deepening
of fidelity to the faith, a fidelity which by now had become largely
linked with fidelity to Mother Ireland. Both fidelities were under
severe pressure and strain; survival itself was a triumph. When
Padraic Colum stood gazing at the Irish College in Paris it was
that spirit of survival which struck him more than anything else:

> Our order broken, they who were our brood
> Knew not themselves the heirs of noted masters,
> Of Columbanus and Eriugena.
>
> We strove towards no high reach of speculation
> Towards no delivery of gestated dogma
> No resolution of age-long disputes.
>
> Only to have a priest beside the hedges,
> Baptising, marrying,
> Offering Mass within some clod-built chapel,
> And to the dying the last sacraments
> Conveying; no more we strove to do –
> We are bare exiles, soldiers, scholars, priests.[66]

CHAPTER 4

'Catholicism of the Irish Kind'

The fusion of Irishness and Catholicity consequent upon the politico-religious persecution, gave Irish Catholicism a sense of itself as independent of any broader historical context.[1] 'It was assumed *a priori*,' writes Desmond Fennell, 'by themselves (the Irish) and others, that they were not primarily human beings involved in modern Anglo-Saxon culture and late Tridentine Catholicism but primarily, in an over-riding sort of way, 'Irish Catholics', – which could mean whatever you wanted it to mean.'[2] It is unfortunate that of all the fifteen hundred years of Christianity in Ireland, its public image, so to speak, should have been taken from the nineteenth century, which in many ways was probably the least *Irish* and indeed the least *Catholic*.

In this chapter I shall endeavour to outline briefly some of the key factors involved in the making of Irish Catholicism from the late eighteenth century to the late twentieth – a phenomenon which some Continental commentators refer to as 'le catholicisme du type irlandais' – Catholicism of the Irish kind.[3] I shall also treat of some aspects of traditional 'Celtic Spirituality' which survived through the period.

Crucial to an understanding of Irish Catholicism from the late eighteenth century to the mid-twentieth are three factors:

(1) The cultural influence of Anglo-Saxon Puritanism;
(2) The large-scale importation of spiritualities;
(3) The centralisation and 'Romanisation' of the church in Ireland.

(1) The cultural influence of Anglo-Saxon Puritanism

Whether through a spirit of loyalty or a recognition of the *status quo*, the Irish people in general, whether Gaelic stock or foreign settlers, recognised the overlordship of the English king from the Norman invasion onwards. There were rebellions indeed, especially during the Tudor reign of terror, but in the seventeenth century Irish Catholics supported Charles I, fought for James II and, after his defeat, continued loyal to the exiled Stuarts James III and Charles III (*Bonnie Prince Charlie*).

As the eighteenth century progressed, significant developments took place in Ireland. Outright persecution declined. At the same time the Penal Laws became even more effective in relation to land as certain people developed skill in using these unjust laws for further personal gain. Catholics were still debarred from holding government office or entering parliament, and a host of lesser restrictions remained on the statute book.

The situation for Catholics was complicated by the fact that the papacy continued to acknowledge the Stuarts as the legitimate rulers of England and recognised their privileges regarding the appointment of bishops in Ireland. However, the papacy refrained from acknowledging the claims of Charles III (*Bonnie Prince Charlie*), thus effectively creating, in Ireland, a separation of church and state as far as the Catholic Church was concerned. This new situation paved the way for recognition by Catholics of the Hanoverian line in the person of George III who acceded to the throne in 1761.

Even in the earlier part of the the eighteenth century there are examples of towns such as Cork, Limerick, Waterford, Clonmel, Galway and elsewhere, which had a small Catholic middle-class with both muscle and money but no political voice. These were generally traders, particularly in the provisions trade. With developments at the political level, and Rome's move towards recognition of the Hanoverians, this Catholic middle-class expanded. Probably because they were conscious of where political power lay, they also developed an obsequious loyalty to the British Crown, best illustrated perhaps by the

'Address of the Roman Catholick Noblemen and Gentlemen of the Counties of Meath and Westmeath' which appeared in the *London Gazette*, on February 3rd 1761, on the occasion of the accession of George. The memorialists begin by humbly presuming,

> to join in our most affectionate and sincere Affliction to your Majesty's Tears, for the much-lamented Death of your Royal Grandfather; a Death universally deplored by all your mourning Subjects, but not by any, more deeply, or more justly felt, than by your poor and distressed Roman Catholicks... who bear in their Breasts, Monuments of eternal Gratitude, for the Indulgence, Favour and Clemency, which he and his Royal Father were most graciously pleased to extend to them on several Occasions.[4]

What these occasions were, the noble and gentlemanly memorialists do not specify, but go on undaunted:

> And now we raise our flowing Eyes, from the Obsequies of our late good and merciful King, to your Majesty's Throne; where, with unspeakable and heart-felt Joy, we behold all his shining Virtues in your Majesty's Royal Person as hereditary as his Crown.[5]

'It was of the same royal grandfather,' says historian John Brady, 'that Thackery wrote a century later: 'here was one who had neither dignity, learning, morals, nor wit – who tainted a great society by a bad example; who, in youth, manhood, old age, was gross, low and sensual.'[6] Well could Daniel O'Connell, 'The Liberator', prophesy: 'In times to come people will not give me due credit for the winning of Catholic Emancipation, for it will not enter into the mind of man to conceive of what race of slaves I have endeavoured to make men.'[7]

There was more to the above-mentioned address than the sonorous language of the obsequious memorialists. It was the voice of a new breed, a Catholic merchant and propertied class who felt that there was a future for them in Ireland if they would but accept the language and tradition of their masters. The language was English. The tradition was neither Irish nor Catholic, but an Anglo-Saxon puritanical culture which had come to pervade not only English society, but that of America and indeed of the entire English-speaking world.

On the nature and values enshrined in this culture now embraced by the Catholic middle class in Ireland, Desmond Fennell comments:

> [In] the mid-nineteenth century the Liberal writer John Stuart Mill saw 'the two influences which have chiefly shaped the British character since the days of the Stuarts' as 'commercial money-getting business and Religious Puritanism.' Besides 'commercial' and 'puritanical', a full characterisation of the predominant cultural stream in nineteenth century Britain, America, and Australia would have to include: democratic, liberal-utilitarian, anti-intellectual, philistine, isolationist in regard to continental European culture.[8]

With the political destruction of Catholic Ireland and the decline of the Irish language, a whole people was cut adrift from fourteen hundred years of Christian tradition and over two thousand years of language, lore and custom. The people were left therefore without any adequate mode of expression culturally familiar to them. It was in this vacuum that a new kind of Catholicism began to take shape – an ancient Catholic creed expressing itself in the context of an Anglo-Saxon puritanical Protestant culture. Small wonder then that it produced something of a hybrid religiousness, an Anglo-Saxon Protestant Puritanical Catholicism which even to this day defies standard categories: 'le catholicisme du type irlandais' – Catholicism of the Irish kind – indeed.

Not classifying it with the European type of Catholicism is, perhaps, justifiable, but as Dr Fennell points out:

> [It] was not its 'Irishness' that was at stake but the centuries-old contact with English culture, which in the nineteenth century became an immersion. It was by adopting the English language, important elements of English political practice

and of English civil and middle-class morality, that the Irish produced a Catholicism which was European in its roots and yet transcended Europe.[9]

In the question of sexual *mores*, for example, the Irish tradition had been well-balanced until the advent of the Puritans. Indeed, some of its attitudes might be considered overly liberal, evidenced, for example, in the eulogising of Cathal Óg MacManus Maguire in the Annals of Ulster not merely for his high offices, hospitality and scholarly attainment but also as a gem of purity and a turtle dove of chastity.[10] The same Cathal Óg was well known to have fathered over a dozen illegitimate children!

Again, marriage shyness in Ireland, a phenomenon of the late nineteenth and early twentieth centuries, can scarcely be attributed to the *Irishness* in the culture. Rather the reverse if we bear in mind that:

(a) in the mid-eighteenth century, Dr Nicholas Madgett, bishop of Kerry, in his *Constitutiones Ecclesiasticae*, notes that 'girls often marry around or before their twenty-first year;'[11]

(b) that the census figures for the early nineteenth century show a marked tendency towards early marriage among the people;[12]

(c) that Protestants in Ireland have a marriage rate which is lower and later than that of Catholics;[13]

(d) that in the late nineteenth century, the narrow restricting views of Continental European moral theologians came to be applied and enforced in a manner never known on this island.

At this point a reference to another matter concerning culture and religion might be in order. I refer to the oft-quoted term 'Irish Jansenism'. The influence of Jansenism in Ireland through the seventeenth and eighteenth century seems to have been minimal. There are indications of a small amount of concern at times, but as Patrick Corish points out: 'we should be very careful in applying the word 'Jansenistic' to Irish Catholic spirituality, all the more so as it has been conclusively shown that the Irish institutions in France, particularly in Paris, where most of the diocesan clergy were educated, were quite positively anti-Jansenist in the eighteenth century.'[14] Then again, Jansenism, like Gallicanism, became a vague term meaning at times little more than a certain austerity, and austerity has always been a hall-mark of traditional Irish piety. The term 'Irish Jansenism' is misleading. More often than not 'Anglo-Saxon Puritanism' may be a more accurate term. But whatever its source there certainly was a narrowness in priestly formation in Maynooth if it was found necessary to publicly burn, on the basis of their alleged laxity, the theological writings of Alphonsus de Liguori, a saint, a doctor of the church and the patron of moral theologians.

(2) The large-scale importation of spiritualities:

In the eighteenth century a format of prayer and brand of piety was developing which would remain with us down to Vatican II. Catholic in theology, it was disseminated through the medium of English against a backdrop of all-pervading Anglo-Saxon puritanical culture.

For an account of this development it is hard to improve on a brief but learned article by Tomás Uasal de Bhál, written in 1967, from which the following excerpt is taken:

> With the publication of Archbishop Butler's catechism in 1777, religion had acquired the idiom which is still current: the language of prayer had been formulated, and many religious exercises had taken definite shape... Primate O'Reilly's catechism preceded Butler's and held its own ground in Ulster; but Butler's gradually became the standard formulary of Catholic belief and practice for all Ireland and for much of the English-speaking world – at the third plenary Council of Baltimore many of the Fathers were in favour of making Butler the official compendium of Christian doctrine for the United States...
>
> Butler, the second James of his name to be Archbishop of Cashel, was a young man, thirty-five years of age, in 1777,

and lived in a thatched house in Thurles. His contemporaries in the metropolitan centres – Challoner in London, Hay in Edinburgh and Carpenter in Dublin – were older and had already done and were still doing much towards establishing a uniform pattern of prayer and devotion. They were not remiss in posting the paths to paradise, laying down and planting gardens of the soul, and providing prototypes of those keys to heaven which have not yet gone out of use.

The influence of Richard Challoner was supreme. As translator of the Bible he gave our religious literature its peculiar rhythm and cadence. He supplied us with a whole library of spirituality, as popular in Ireland as it was in his own country. His *Garden of the Soul*, first published in 1740, was the ancestor of all our prayer-books. Its subtitle defined its scope: 'a manual of sacred exercises and instructions for Christians who, living in the world, aspire to devotion.' It contained many of the prayers still current... [and] ceremonies that have not since changed, e.g. the ceremony of Benediction of the Blessed Sacrament, are in the *Garden* described for the first time in the English language. It superseded the older and more liturgical prayer-books, the *Primer* and the *Manual*. Much as Challoner himself loved these, they were now relegated to the upper classes while the *Garden* came to terms with the common man, the townsman more perhaps than the countryman, and that was important in the late eighteenth century when a Catholic middle-class began to emerge in the cities and towns of Ireland.

Only less than that of Challoner was the influence of George Hay, vicar-apostolic of the Lowland district of Scotland, in shaping the pattern of prayer and devotion of Irish Catholics of his time.[15]

Hay's publications – *Sincere Christian, Devout Christian, Pious Christian*, etc. – were immensely popular in Ireland. His works enjoyed support from the Irish bishops, especially those of the

Leinster province. The writings of Richard Challoner (1691-
1781) vicar apostolic in the London district from 1741 were,
however, the most popular if we are to judge by the booksellers'
lists. Of his school of thought and life experience Patrick Corish
writes:

> Challoner, and indeed all the other popular authors, were
> quite firmly in the Jesuit and Salesian tradition of spirituality.
> This indicates that one must be very cautious in applying the
> term 'Jansenistic' to the severe and anxious strain which un-
> doubtedly developed in Irish middle-class Catholic spiritual-
> ity in the eighteenth century. It is true that a severe and anx-
> ious spirituality was now the dominant characteristic of
> French Jansenism, and it is likewise true that by far the
> greater number of the Irish clergy now received their theo-
> logical formation in France, but the Irish institutions there
> had a record of opposition to Jansenism, and while the clergy
> undoubtedly returned with some Gallican leanings, the
> Jansenist strain must have been slight. The anxious severity
> that developed in Irish Catholicism must rather be traced to
> the devotional reading available in English. Challoner him-
> self does retain much of the serenity and humanism of his
> master, St Francis de Sales, but a sadder note runs through
> his writings, beyond doubt the fruit of his experiences as a
> bishop in penal-day London. Catholic life in penal-day
> Dublin was also a saddening experience, and it is not surpris-
> ing that Irish Catholics found Challoner congenial, for they
> lived under the same conditions as he did.[16]

Thus began the wholesale importation of books and booklets of
Catholic piety into Ireland.

Aside from the reason given by Corish for their popularity, a
good part of the success of British religious publications in
Ireland was due to lack of competition from the Irish side. It was
not that the Irish lacked spirituality: they lacked language in
which to express it. English, the new medium, could not express
either in depth or accuracy the Gaelic approach to God. Over the

centuries the Irish language and culture had become thoroughly imbued with Christian and Catholic sentiment, whereas, in an oft-quoted phrase of an old Cork Capuchin, 'the English language is the language of heresy'. In the nineteenth-century Irish scene it certainly was. The problem, of course, was not the English language itself but the culture which it had come to embody.

However, despite the good Capuchin's assertion, it must be acknowledged that the language of the towns had always been English and the towns, with the exception of Carrickfergus, remained staunchly loyal to the Catholic faith and developed a piety which was adequate. We must also bear in mind that the townspeople who shared the Catholic faith with their Gaelic rural neighbours neither aspired to nor achieved a cultural integration with them.

The bishops in the late eighteenth and early nineteenth centuries were confronted with a difficult choice: should Irish or English be chosen as the medium for handing on the faith? On the one hand, the traditional vehicle, Irish language and culture, was in decline; while on the other, English, the language of an expanding empire, had the tide in its favour. Most of the bishops sailed with that tide, though not always without feelings of perplexity.

John Carpenter, Archbishop of Dublin and an able scholar and lover of the Gaelic language, published a *Rituale* in 1776 containing instructions on religious matters in simple Irish. Faced with the problem of governing a traditionally English-speaking diocese, however, and seeing such an output of spiritual writing in that language, he seems to have lost heart or judged it better to let the move towards English take its course.

Britain wasn't the only source of new spirituality for the Irish. The Continent was an equally prominent source. From France, Belgium, Italy and elsewhere poured in new approaches, new ideas, new religious orders and societies of one kind or another, each with its own brand of piety and accompanying badge, medal or holy chord. Spiritual nosegays and particular examens, Francis de Sales and Pere Grou, processions and sparkling shrines – all began to figure in the Irish spiritual diet; as did jubilees, tridua, novenas, missions, 'Forty Hours', perpetual adoration, blessed altars, Benediction, stations of the cross, devotions to the Sacred Heart and to the Immaculate Conception, confraternities, sodalities, societies of many brands – Vincent de Paul, Temperance, Purgatorian. Along with these came the back-up material – scapulars, missals, prayer-books, medals, holy pictures, *Agnus Dei*, prayers that never fail to be answered, and, of course, Rosary beads.

It was not that these elements were totally lacking in the country. The Rosary had long been part of the tradition. There is record of Rinuccini, the papal nuncio in 1647 not only giving his blessing to all in St Nicholas' Collegiate Church, Galway, but also his ordering of Exposition of the Blessed Sacrament to take place in the churches of the city and hinterland and the holding of the Forty Hours Adoration. A few years later (1652) and long before St Margaret Mary's visions, Oliver Cromwell's chaplain wrote a theological work on devotion to the Sacred Heart, but the book seems not to have made such a strong impression on Ireland as Cromwell himself did![17]

The good intentions of those who introduced the new devotional practices is beyond question. Nor was there anything particularly *wrong* with the practices themselves; they were simply inadequate to, and often out of tune with, the culture and religious sensibilities of the broad mass of the Gaelic people. For a summary comment on the switch from the old piety to the new, Tomás de Bhál again:

> So it comes that down to our own time our piety has been of the eighteenth century, Georgian in style and pattern rather than Gothic or Gaelic; our formal praying has been, so to speak, a kind of period-piece, more suited to the squares and broad streets of Dublin than to the Irish countryside...

> One is loth to be critical of so venerable a corpus of prayer and piety but may one most respectfully suggest that it may

be too sustained where it should be a little more sponta-
neous, too civilised and urban where it should be a bit
bedraggled and daring and rural, too elaborate where it
should be inspired, too flat and level where it should be soar-
ing to the skies, too articulate and too fully stated for the
Celtic mentality for which, as Kuno Meyer said, the 'half-said
thing is dearest'.[18]

(3) The centralisation and 'Romanisation' of the church in Ireland:

That the Church in Ireland needed some special attention and
reform after the chaotic era of persecution goes without saying.
The faith itself was strong but there were weaknesses in structure and discipline. Among the clergy there was still much pettiness and squabbling; and dissension was prevalent among the
hierarchy, particularly on the vexed question of what stand it
should take vis-a-vis the British government's educational policies for Ireland. With the advent of Catholic Emancipation in
1829 the church was free to devote itself to reorganising and re-
structuring. In the words of Desmond Fennell: 'The new Irish
church was almost totally unencumbered by dead baggage or
by mortgages from the past and was very poor, materially and
culturally. There was not even an *ancien régime* in the background for reactionaries to hark back to or for progressives to
use as a bogeyman. Modern Irish Catholicism had the freedom
and strength which youth and poverty offer. Because it was rich
in faith it was able to use them.'[19]

Rich in faith it was. The strong-arm tactics of persecution
yielded a poor harvest to the Reformed church. There were
those after Emancipation who believed that the velvet glove
could succeed where the iron fist had failed. Taking advantage
of the poverty and famine in the land, they roamed the country
with 'a Bible in one hand and a soup ticket in the other'.[20] Yet
the census of 1861 revealed that their effort was largely futile.[21]

In October 1851, Michael Jones, a former student of
Propaganda's Urban College in Rome, complained to Cardinal
Franzoni: 'The Irish people are very good, but much neglected

in every way by both the Civil and Ecclesiastical Government, more by the latter than the former.'[22] Jones might have done well to withhold his complaint, because already in 1850 two significant events had happened – events destined to transform the face of Irish Catholicism. The first of these was the appointment of Paul Cullen to the vacant primatial see of Armagh; the second, the national Synod of Thurles – the first of its kind in Ireland since the twelfth century.

Dr Cullen had spent thirty years in Rome as a student, professor in Propaganda College, vice-rector of the Irish College, Roman Procurator of the Irish and Australian Bishops, and in 1849, *rector pro tempore* of Propaganda College. He was well aware of the Irish scene and shared the anxiety of the Holy See over the disunity that was evident among the Irish hierarchy. His standing with the Roman authorities was such that his advice was sought, not only on Irish affairs but on many other matters as well.

A man who had 'become imbued with the current Roman outlook,'[23] Cullen was a devoted bishop, anxious only to promote the welfare of the Catholic Church; a tireless champion of the poor, an able organiser and administrator, and an advocate of strict ecclesiastical discipline. Always a firm opponent of political violence, he nevertheless took a strictly independent attitude to government and civic administration. He regarded the role of bishops and priests as one of spiritual service to their flocks and strongly emphasised the value of ecclesiastical obedience of priests to bishops and of bishops to the Pope. He ensured that the instructions and decisions of Propaganda were based on the fullest knowledge of the Irish situation and he then set himself to carry out the policy of the Holy See as faithfully as possible.[24]

The Synod of Thurles, the second event marking out 1850 as a turning point in the history of the Irish Church, sat between August 22nd and September 10th. The scope of its activity was wide, as indicated by its one hundred and eighty-nine decrees on eleven separate topics: faith, sacraments (with the exception of holy orders), the life of the clergy, the keeping of archives, church property, education (two sections), and clerical dissensions.[25] Present in his dual capacity as leader of the Irish hierarchy and apostolic delegate of Pius IX, Dr Cullen hoped that the synod would 'lay the foundation of a good and general system of Canon Law for the Irish Church,'[26] and on this foundation he was to strive for the rest of his life to build an organised and disciplined church, governed by a united and disciplined hierarchy.

Cullen's success as a reformer was in no small measure due to his considerable personal skills as an ecclesiastical politician, combined with the strong support of Rome, especially in the matter of episcopal appointments. Referring to the kind of candidates put forward by Cullen to fill episcopal sees in Ireland, Emmet Larkin says:

> In general Cullen preferred to promote men... who were made in his own image and likeness. They were not only good preachers, adequate theologians, zealous, courageous enough, and young, but they were also generally strangers to the diocese and, therefore, they did not have any of the personal ties or loyalties that might inhibit them in their zeal for reform. If they were not recruited from the regular clergy, moreover, the new bishops were usually rectors or vice-rectors of seminaries – strict, stern, austere men who had both the experience of, and a proven talent for, effective administration. They were also well aware that the new discipline they represented would not be popular among their priests, but if these bishops were ever to make their wills effective with their clergy, the bishops would have to depend on their patron's continued exertions on their behalf at Rome. They all tended, therefore, to be ultramontanes because Rome was not only the theoretical but the actual source of their own and Cullen's real power in the Irish Church.[27]

In the eyes of the bishops the main clerical vices were wine, women and avarice. Lust and drunkenness, especially the latter, might be tolerated by the people as weakness, but, in the words of Bishop Moriarty of Kerry, 'avarice they never pardon either in life or death; it is for them as the sin against the Holy Ghost... who shall not be forgiven neither in this world nor in the world to come (Mt 12:32).'[28] Moriarty further reminds his clergy that 'no amount of piety, no integrity of life, no seeming zeal, no labour in the work of the priesthood, will gain for an avaricious man the goodwill of the people.'[29]

As always in the face of problems that refuse to go away, the people resort to the usual palliatives of humour and satire. The language and lore of the nation abound with tales of clerical greed. The story is still in the oral tradition of the Cork-Kerry border of an encounter between Eoghan Rua Ó Súilleabháin, the poet, and the parish priest and curate of Rathmore. It is told that the two priests were out for a walk when who should come along the road but Eoghan. The curate said to his companion, 'Let's have a bit of fun at the expense of Eoghan Rua.' So when the parties met, the curate, who happened to spot a raven by the roadside, said: 'You are a very learned man Eoghan; will you tell me when will the raven talk?' Aware of the facetious nature of the question the witty poet replied:

Nuair a thiocfaidh an míol-mór ar an Maing,
Nuair a thiocfaidh an Fhrainc go Sliabh Mís,
Nuair a chaillfhidh an sagart a' t-saint,
Ansin a thiocfaidh an caint do'n bhfiachdubh.

(When the whale comes up the River Main,
When France comes to Slieve Mish,
when the priest loses his greed,
Then will the raven talk.)

'You got your answer!' said the parish priest to his humbled curate, and Eoghan went his way.

Associated with the problem of avarice was the custom of celebrating the sacraments of baptism, eucharist, penance and matrimony in private houses. While the custom probably had its origins in the exigencies of penal days, it was alleged that its continuation was for a less worthy motive: more lucrative pickings for the clergy.[30] When the reforming National Synod of Thurles addressed this question the pastoral custom of holding 'stations' bore the brunt of the attack.

Stations, which may have originated in the penal days or earlier, was a practice well-suited to an Irish tradition of intimate communities. A parish was divided into 'station areas' and every spring and autumn the local priests visited every station area where, in a designated house chosen on a basis of rotation, the priests heard confessions, celebrated Mass and distributed Holy Communion. The stations were a godsend to the people, especially the feeble and the elderly who had little chance of walking four, eight, or more miles over rough terrain to the nearest church.

Complaints were made about the wretchedness of the houses where the Holy Mass was celebrated,[31] and about the financial burden to the family concerned and the priest's attitude in this regard,[32] but the real stumbling-block as far as Rome was concerned was the custom of hearing women's confessions 'outside of the place for confession'.[33] It seems that many Continentals, and those Irish churchmen imbued with the Roman spirit, could scarcely envisage a priest being alone with a woman without sin on the part of either or both. Cullen would settle for nothing less than the abolition of hearing women's confessions outside of the confessional as is evident from his rejection of the mild decree passed by the Synod of Thurles.[34] He pointed out to Propaganda that hearing confessions of women in private houses was 'full of dangers for priests, especially young priests'.[35] Cullen's uncle, Fr Maher, had no doubts about the problem: 'The young clergyman is brought in contact with his female penitents. The result is confessions are often invalid or sacrilegious.'[36]

Stations were finally outlawed by Rome but persisted in several Irish dioceses – especially in the south and west. Their survival is, I think, a healthy sign, a triumph of the *sensus fidelium*, for they were good pastoral practice not merely for 'reconciling sinners and distributing the bread of life' but also for 'eliminating any scandals they [the priests] come across, healing dissensions, cultivating friendship and charity with all, and exercising the role of counsellor.'[37] Ironically, in the post-Vatican II church, stations and house-masses are officially promoted and encouraged world-wide.

Though devotional reform proceeded apace, further romanising and centralising the Irish church, some of the old customs and anarchies – giving expression to the Dionysian element in humanity – persisted, in spite of clerical disapproval. In his book *Three Days on the Shannon*, W. F. Wakeman, the nineteenth-century antiquarian, gives a first hand account of the pilgrimage to Clonmacnoise in the middle of the nineteenth century:

> Upon his return to the churches by the road, he (the traveller) will have an opportunity of visiting the holy well of St Kieran, upon whose patron day (the 24th September) an immense concourse of pilgrims from the surrounding counties, and even from more distant places, assemble at Clonmacnoise for the purpose of doing penance. Nothing can be more singular than the appearance of the people when on their rounds, visiting the various stations where it is customary to say certain prayers, or perform acts of penance. The devotees come in hundreds, leading with them the lame, the halt, and the blind, who, notwithstanding the Roman Catholic clergy all over the country have very generally set their faces against the continuation of 'Patterns', and even forbid their flocks to attend them, will still come, believing that through divine grace, and the intercession of the saints, or through the particular favour of the local saint, they may be relieved of their infirmities upon their doing penance and performing certain rites. These customs have degenerated very generally into scenes of debauchery, having been discountenanced by the clergy. Still, however, people will assemble, and tents for sale of whiskey and refreshments are erected notwithstanding the efforts which have been made to suppress such meetings.[38]

One response to the undoubted abuse of alcohol was the extraordinarily effective Temperance Movement begun in the late

1830's by a young Capuchin Friar, Theobald Mathew. Mainly through his zealous preaching, the consumption of alcohol fell by more than half between 1839 and 1844.[39]

There was a wonderful popular response to the jubilee year of 1826. 'In Dublin at any rate,' says Patrick Corish, 'the jubilee might be described as the first parish mission. In every church there was instruction in the early morning, and again at midday and in the evening. Confessions were continuous, and the days of general communion with renewal of baptismal vows turned into a public proclamation of faith.'[40]

Of the Carlow Mission in 1843, an eyewitness declared: 'Hundreds remained all night in the chapel, and many remained in town away from their homes for five or six days waiting an opportunity for confessing.'[41] Of the same Mission, Paul Cullen's sister, Margaret, wrote to him that it 'would be impossible for me to describe the enthusiasm of the people. If the missioners were angels from heaven, they could not be more venerated.' She described how work was at a standstill, while people followed the missioners around all day and crowded 'in hundreds to the confessionals, many, very many who had never before been there.' The missioners preached three times a day in the chapel, which was 'crowded to suffocation.' 'What a pity,' she concluded, 'we have not more priests in the parish.'[42]

Nine years later, Cullen, now Archbishop of Dublin, wrote to Fr Kirby, his successor in the Irish College: 'Here we are trying to enroll a large missionary body before next summer to wipe out the proselytisers everywhere... The Jesuits, Dominicans, Carmelites, Vincentians, Redemptorists, secular Priests will all join together.'[43]

The work of popular renewal continued and the people flocked to missions and devotions, whether preached by men with a French, Italian, Belgian, British, Dutch or Russian accent. The people were moulded into a thoroughly sacramental and Mass-going church. In half a century or so[44] the Mass attendance increased from an estimated 30-40% to over 90% and thus it remained until the 1980s.

The revival and reorganisation of church life in nineteenth century Ireland was a magnificent achievement at many levels – in the renewal of structures, the training of clergy, the building of churches, the expansion of religious orders, the flourishing of popular devotions. But of course the truly wonderful element in all this was the people's response to the reforms – an enthusiastic response that betokened vast reserves of faith in their hearts. The pity is that the zealous and well-intentioned reforming churchmen failed to recognise, and indeed often actively suppressed, the age-old native spirituality with its linguistic and ritual expressions that had developed organically from the time of St Patrick and had endured through centuries 'of dungeon, fire and sword.'

When *le catholicisme du type irlandais* became the predominant expression of the Catholic faith in Ireland towards the end of the nineteenth century, there was bitter disappointment in the heart of many a cleric and lay person who was sharp enough to realise what was really happening. Fr Walter Conway of Glenamaddy, Co Galway, expressed his disappointment at the supplanting of a tradition:

> The prayers and the Religious Poems which our ancestors composed and used to repeat, have been given up... pieces which came from the heart of him who composed them, and which went straight from the heart of him who said them to the ear of God. And what have we in their place? *Ráiméis* [i.e. nonsense] which half of those who repeat it do not understand, and from which they reap neither fruit nor profit.[45]

Since the Second Vatican Council (1962-1965) the 'Catholicism of the Irish kind' is gradually declining, but in that decline we may rediscover a more enduring link with the wider and deeper tradition of Irish spirituality. I often wonder if Austin Clarke is not grappling with this very point in *Emancipation*:[46]

> That wretched girl still wakes me up
> At night, for all she wore had been thrown
> Away. I see her by O'Connell Bridge

> And think: 'Yes, more than a century
> Ago, religion went in such rags here.'
> But pity is a kind of lust,
> Although it stretch and turn. Have I
> Not found at last what covers mine,
> In the cast-off finery of faith?

Some would say that two spiritualities contended in nineteenth century Ireland and that unfortunately the wrong one, the one that was never quite in tune with the Irish soul and sensibility, prevailed. In many of his poems Clarke lamented, often bitterly, this sad fact and its twentieth century consequences.

CHAPTER 5

'Fasting like an Irishman'

In October 1790, a Frenchman, Charles Etienne Coquebert de Montbret, paid a visit to Kerry and the south-west. Coquebert was no ordinary tourist, but a brilliant scholar and an experienced investigator. An edited version of his diary is now available and makes interesting reading.[1] Coquebert is convinced that the Catholic religion, 'a religion that encourages politeness and lenience,'[2] plays a big part in forming the character of the people:

> The goodness of these people reveals itself in their love of children and in their kindness to strangers. When they give charity they do so with an air of politeness to avoid humiliating the recipient, and the best place at the fire is reserved for the poor man. They are full of imagination and quick to understand what one wants to know. If they lack the required information, they straight away invent a story to provide an answer, where in a similar case a German would just keep on saying *ich weiss nicht, ich weiss nicht*, ten times.[3]

Coquebert goes on to compare the Irish and the English:

> The native Irish are very different from the people of England. When an Englishman grows wealthy he has no desire to expend money in proportion to his increased wealth. From peer to shopkeeper the English all live in almost the same way – snug and comfortable. But in Ireland as in France every man increases his expenditure in proportion to his profits. The Irish are also more friendly than the English and are far more anxious to acquire knowledge. The people of

Munster have a passionate desire for learning and spare nothing to give their children the best possible education, according to their means. Formerly every fairly well-to-do family kept a Latin master in its house and all the children in the neighbourhood were taught by him.[4]

A beautiful illustration of the inventive courtesy mentioned by Coquebert is related of a Kerry priest in the nineteenth century who, in his pastoral visitation during the Great Famine, consoled the living and buried the dead. Speaking to a woman who had lost her twin boys – boys well-loved by the old priest – he tried to hold back the tears as he spoke words of comfort to the distraught mother:

'You see, Máire, God wanted the pair, and the high angel, Michael, marked them to fill two grand places and to prepare places for you and their father who is working down in Limerick. There they are this minute, Donnchadh O'Shea [the departed piper] playing *Bó na leath-adhairce* for them, and the Glorious Maiden herself bringing them around, one by each hand, to meet the old neighbours, all talking about the Regatta at the Pattern and the fine rowing of the Fearanniarach boys. And they must also help the thrushes to build their nests there, and tumble about with the young hares. You musn't be weeping Máire.' 'I see the tears running down your own face Father,' replied the mother, but the kindly priest continued to hide his own grief: 'It's only the mountain mist, only the mountain mist, Máire.'[5]

A contemporary of Coquebert, the Englishman Arthur Young, did a tour of Ireland about the same time and was struck by the 'vivacity and a great and eloquent volubility of speech... They are infinitely more cheerful and lovely than anything we commonly see in England, having nothing of that incivility of sullen silence, with which so many enlightened Englishmen seem to wrap themselves up, as if retiring within their own importance.'[6]

Arthur Young expounds on some further qualities of the Irish. They are, he says:

> so spiritedly active at play that, at hurling, which is the cricket of savages, they show the greatest feats of agility. Their love for society is as remarkable as their curiosity is insatiable; and their hospitality to all comers, be their own poverty ever so pinching, has too much merit to be forgotten. Pleased to enjoyment with a joke, or witty repartee, they will repeat it with such expression, that the laugh will be universal... dancing is so universal among them that there are everywhere itinerant dancing masters, to whom the cottars pay six-pence a quarter for teaching their families.[7]

Irish hospitality extended no less to the dead than to the living. It is still with us and has always been characteristic of our religious expression. There was a widespread belief, for instance, that the dead members of the family visited their old home at the beginning of November, the ancient pagan Irish feast of *Samhain* from which the Christian celebrations of *All Saints* and *All Souls* seem to have derived. Leaving the door unlocked, having a good fire in the hearth, and the placing of a bowl of water on the table was a common mode of preparing the house for a visit from the dead at *Samhain*. So too was the custom of lighting a candle for each deceased family member – a ritual performed during evening prayer in the home. Kevin Danaher, the folklorist, once asked an old man if he was in dread of entering a haunted house. 'In dread of it?' replied the old man. 'What would I be in dread of, and the souls of my own dead as thick as bees around me?'[8] Having offered Mass at home on *Samhain Night* I said to my aged father: 'They were all there tonight.' 'They were,' he replied with a perfect understanding, as if I had been referring to a congregation of the living, but at that Mass the only visible persons present were himself and one of my sisters. Whether people were 'alive' or 'dead' made little difference to him, for he was of a tradition that drew no hard and fast lines between life in *gleann na ndeor*, the vale of tears, or *Tir na nóg*, the Land of the Young – heaven.

One of the loveliest descriptions of a family at prayer on All Souls Night comes from a Co Limerick farmhouse in the late nineteenth century. It was the one night in the year on which the rosary was not said by the O'Connor family at Lough Gur. There was a special ritual for that night:

> Father drew his chair and mother's into the middle of the kitchen, for this was the one night of the year when we did not say the rosary; we children moved near to them and Dinny-bawn sat on the floor at father's feet; the servants drew out the forms and knelt against them with the fiddler and Murnane. When the shuffling of feet quietened and the room was still, father read the litany of the dead: very solemn and lonely it was. We made the responses in hushed voices as if we were listening for the rustling of home-faring souls. Father prayed for his own dead and for mother's by name... 'my father, Michael, Thy Servant... Mammy Mac and Mammy Jug, Thy Servants, Catherine and Joanna,' for 'the lord' and other departed friends. He did not forget Ellie's and Bridgie's parents, nor Murnane's wife. He prayed for 'Dick Dooley, my faithful friend and helper,' and for Tom Hickey's father, and for those whom the wandering fiddler had loved and lost. Last of all he prayed for Dinny-Bawn's Mary:
>
> > Eternal rest grant to them, O Lord,
> > And may perpetual light shine upon them.[9]

Liturgical changes in the nineteen-sixties – temporarily I expect – dampened the celebration of the feast of *Samhain*, at least that aspect of it which pays special honour to the dead. In more recent times the government changed the public holiday from the feast itself to the last Monday in October. These blows from both the religious and secular authorities has weakened the awareness of the riches of the festival, and what was a celebration of hope and joy and communion has degenerated into consumerist nonsense about witches and skeletons. Then too, because we are losing touch with nature and its seasonal cycles, the incongruous notion of having a 'cemetery Sunday' in the middle of

Summer is evolving. *Samhain,* celebrated at a time when all of nature is dying or dead and the cycle of the year is ended, is surely the more appropriate time for such remembrances. However the *Samhain* tradition is so deep that rebuilding it may not be difficult when a proper sense of things begins to reassert itself.

Pilgrimage is another expression of the faith of the people which has survived the nineteenth century and is presently regaining popularity. The pilgrimage phenomenon has always been quite extraordinary, and a high percentage of modern Irish have been on pilgrimage of one kind or another either at home or overseas.

The most famous pilgrim shrines at home are Knock, Croagh Patrick and Lough Derg. Among others less frequented but still popular are Faughart, Glendalough, Lady's Island, Ballyvourney, Clonmacnoise, and Ballyheigue. The pattern of pilgrimage to foreign parts has changed somewhat. No longer included in the general run of foreign pilgrimages are Compostella or Iona, but bigger numbers than ever are going to Rome and the Holy Land, as well as to the Continental Marian shrines, notably Fatima and Lourdes and, recently, Medjugorgje. This list in no way exhausts the catalogue of shrines frequented each year by Irish Pilgrims.

Of the Irish pilgrim-centres, Knock, Co Mayo, attracts by far the greatest number of pilgrims in any given year. As a place of devotion it is of relatively recent origin. In 1879 the Mother of God and other heavenly personalities are said to have appeared there. Since then it has grown in popularity becoming the National Marian Shrine. Despite the building of a spacious basilica there, the windswept landscape has retained much of its native character, and the warm spirit and faith of the pilgrims is inspiring. A curious feature of the Knock pilgrim ritual is that 'doing the rounds' goes anti-clockwise, i.e. the direction for *cursing* rather than *blessing* in the Irish tradition! A change of direction would bring it into line with the age-old tradition of walking *deiseal* (clockwise) rather than *tuathail* (anticlockwise or 'widdershins' in Scotland) round the shrine.

A Romanian priest, Fr John Filip, visiting the shrine in 1956, noted:

> ... the pilgrim throng that encircled the church quietly reciting the rosary or devoutly kneeling at the oratory of the apparition. It is here one comes into direct contact with the very soul of Ireland... at Knock one is struck in a special way by the cordiality and warm family-spirit which pervades and with which the invalids are treated and ministered to by the good Handmaids and stewards who fulfil their wonderful apostolate with great faith and a deep spirit of sacrifice.[10]

That his observations are equally true of Knock half a century later I can personally vouch for. It continues to be a power-house of prayer, a centre of community worship for the people of the land, a spot where people with a traditional love for Jesus and his mother can pour their hearts out with freedom of spirit. Time and again I have observed groups and individuals of all ages pray at Knock – engaged couples, newly-weds, whole families, multitudes of people from every class and background, bound in one set purpose. And how they pray! Heart and soul goes into that pilgrimage: the stations of the cross, the 'rounds'[11], the contemplation of the life, death and resurrection of Christ in the fifteen mysteries of the rosary. Finally, the climax of the day, the Eucharist. No fun and games here, no distractions except the frequent rain which is accepted as God's gift and incorporated, usually with humour and laughter, into the penitential aspect of the day.

Contrasting the penances involved in making the other two national pilgrimages – Croagh Patrick and Lough Derg – often provides material for small talk and divergence of views. For myself Lough Derg is the more daunting but it is really a matter of personal preference – whether to starve and go sleepless over a number of days, or whether to go barefoot up the slopes of a rocky mountain and get the penance over in a matter of five to seven hours.

Both Lough Derg and Croagh Patrick are shrines associated

with the national apostle. In each place he is said to have prayed and fasted forty days and forty nights. The former (St Patrick's Purgatory) is the tiny island shrine in Co Donegal. The latter, popularly known as 'The Reek' (from its shape), is a hulk of quartz in Co Mayo that dominates the north Connacht horizons. The use of the word 'mountain' is relative of course. Croagh Patrick is a mere 2,510 feet high; yet, when climbing it in bare feet or on bare knees, a pilgrim is entirely justified in seeing it as a lofty mountain.

To the present day people of all ages climb 'The Reek'. The pilgrimage may be done at any time of year, but that held on 'Reek Sunday' – the last Sunday in July – has a long tradition behind it. Indeed, there is very strong evidence to suggest that the Gaels had resorted here for religious purposes long before St Patrick gave it a Christian orientation.[12] The night Vigil of Reek Sunday is the traditional time for undertaking the climb, and on that July night a vast throng makes the ascent, an estimated twenty thousand during the Vigil and perhaps up to fifty thousand in the course of the year. Fifty thousand people out of a population of about four million Catholics is a large percentage, particularly striking when one considers that the pilgrimage is undertaken without any formal organisation by the institutional church.

I once met a young man on the slopes of that mountain. He was an agnostic from Sweden who had come to immerse himself in the faith of the Irish pilgrims in the hope of finding for himself a new understanding of life. He found it extremely difficult to understand the penitential aspect – the bare feet and the sight of some clinging to the age-old custom of climbing on bare knees. But failure to understand penance is failure to understand Irish Christianity. Suffering with the gentle Christ who suffered for us is integral to the tradition.

As chaplain to a pilgrimage of young people in their late teens and early twenties, I was gaily tripping along the foothills when I noticed that I was virtually alone in wearing shoes. I speedily and quietly cast them aside and entered into the full spirit of the pilgrimage, becoming aware as I did so of how I had been so much part of an institution which had distanced itself from the living popular tradition. In later pilgrimages I have often watched pilgrims in their penitential climb: no compulsion here, no embarrassment, just simple voluntary happy choice. As a phenomenon of the last quarter of the twentieth century, as of ages past, such a religious expression is a decided sign of hope as well as of continuity.

For pilgrims to Lough Derg, there is often a journey of five, perhaps even ten, hours by coach and, for some, an overnight stop *en route*. In all, it involves three days (seventy-two hours) fasting. The only concession made to human weakness is one meal of dry toast and black tea taken while on the island. One is also permitted some 'Lough Derg Soup', a concoction which one pilgrim assured me was made from the simplest of recipes: hot water and pepper.

Even before landing on the island, pilgrims must remove all shoes and stockings. The sharp loose stones which form the surface of the island provide an excellent opportunity for mortification as the pilgrims hobble about 'doing the beds.' The beds in this instance are the various graves and shrines of Celtic saints. No sleep is allowed during the first night on the island and if the preacher's words send the pilgrims peacefully into the arms of Morpheus there is always a kind (or envious?) friend at hand to ensure that the embrace is not prolonged.

Lough Derg is highly institutionalised, but underneath, there persists the real surging piety of the people. There are pilgrims who return again and again, perhaps as often as twenty or even forty times, usually at intervals of a year.

To sum up Lough Derg it is hard to do better than quote a snippet of conversation I once overheard in Dr Pádraig Ó Domhnaill's waiting-room in Rathfarnham, Dublin:

Mrs A: You'd want to be frightfully fit for it.
Mrs B: You come out refreshed in mind and heart and body.
Mrs A: Is it still very rough?
Miss C: Yes, and I believe what they say about sharpening the stones at night!

At provincial and parochial level pilgrimages are legion. The Marian Grotto at Ballyheigue in Co Kerry is what amounts to Kerry's County Shrine. Here, year after year, on Mary's birthday, September 8th, thousands of people come to pray. By long-standing tradition adult sons and daughters who have left the locality are duty-bound to return home to take parents or other relatives to the shrine. When I myself made the pilgrimage, the parish priest assured me that this custom is still observed as a sacred trust.

At least twice a year the little town of Ballyvourney in Co Cork is thronged to capacity as pilgrims come to the ancient shrine and well of St Gobnait. Again, as at other wells and shrines, the pilgrims are not limited to making their visits on those days only. A holy well or shrine is a spot for prayer at any time. The Ballyvourney shrine has been restored in recent years and a limestone statue, executed by the late and much loved Seámus Murphy, crowns the hallowed spot. The prayer at the base of the statue is in the traditional mould – simple, direct, straight from the heart. Mr John Lucey, a local shopkeeper, sent it to me along with many other beautiful prayers in use among the people of the district:

> Go mbeannaí Dia dhuit a Ghobnait Naofa,
> Go mbeannaí Muire dhuit is beannaím féin duit.
> Is chughatsa a thánag, ag gearán mo scéil leat,
> Is ag iarraidh mé a leigheas ar son Dé ort.

> (May God bless you St Gobnait!
> May Mary bless you! And I greet you myself too.
> It is to you I have come telling you my story,
> And asking you for God's sake to heal me).

The Irish pilgrimage incorporates many elements of the religious tradition: the penitential element, the prescribed patterns of prayer (usually of a repetitive nature), the element of repentance and conversion, intercession for one's own needs and for the Body of Christ, the church. There is also a lovely freedom associated with the outdoors and the closeness to nature: on the wild mountain, as on Brandon; in the wooded valley, as in Glendalough; on the lake-island, as in Gougane Barra; or amid the luxuriant pastureland around St Mullins in Co Carlow. Another feature is the vigil, a religious practice dear to the Irish of all ages, not only because of scriptural precedents but because we are 'people of the night'. And there is that ever-present pere-grinatory passion: it is always sweeter to make a pilgrimage than to say one's prayers at home.

Finally, humour is rarely lacking. People from the south-west love to relate how the Bishop of Kerry led a pilgrimage to the top of Mount Brandon on May 16th, St Brendan's Feast. Brandon Mountain is engulfed in rain and cloud for most of the year. On this particular day the bleak summit was lashed by bit-ing wind and driving cold rain. As the assembled multitude proclaimed the mystery of faith, 'Christ has died, Christ is risen, Christ will come again', one disenchanted pilgrim was distinctly heard to proclaim 'Christ, I won't come again!'

I believe that gain or loss in the future will depend greatly on how the penitential side of Irish faith is cultivated. An elderly confrere who had done his seminary training in Paris contrasted for me in a homely way the difference between Irish and French spirituality. He spoke in concrete, colourful language and re-ferred to the French leaning towards introspection and particu-lar examens and the like: 'It is not natural for the Irishman to take his spiritual temperature,' said he, 'but quite natural for him to starve himself, or beat hell out of himself.' The same priest assured me that 'fasting like an Irishman' was an expres-sion current on the Continent in the seventeenth century.

Certainly this penitential element is dear to Irish piety today, not only in conjunction with pilgrimages, but in many other as-pects of devotion. In a school retreat which I conducted, one of the exercises I requested was communal penance: in this case each young student kneeling on the hands for the duration of five *Paters*, *Aves* and *Glorias* with the intention of making repara-tion to Christ for the sins of the world. The students joyfully and generously undertook this exercise amid a tumult of 'ohs' and 'aahs'. Six years later the teacher in charge informed me that the pupils, now adults, still remembered with satisfaction what had been for them a telling religious experience.

Fasting, 'starving oneself' as my friend Geoffrey O'Connell put it, survives at least residually. After the reforms of the Second Vatican Council when lay readers were introduced in the Sunday Liturgy, a Co Cork woman was asked to read the Word of God on the following Sunday. She acceded to the request, but as a 'natural' preliminary to the reading she fasted all day on Saturday. Her entire traditional piety came to the fore: what she was undertaking was a solemn event: she would stand before the people – her people – and proclaim the Word of God; deep preparation was called for, a rinsing of body and soul.

Still on the theme of fasting, another deep-rooted Irish instinct is to practise fasting as an expression of one's inner convictions and values. It manifests itself dramatically in the form of the hunger-strike. The hunger-strike in early Christian and pre-Christian Ireland was used as a means of obtaining redress or strengthening one's bargaining power with God or man. It is still basically that: an assertion of a person's sincerely-held convictions against the official authoritative assessment of the situation. It was during the Irish War of Independence when Terence MacSwiney, the Lord Mayor of Cork, fasted to death in Brixton prison, London in 1920, that theologians around the world got seriously interested in developing a theology of hunger-strike as a legitimate means of resisting oppression.

In recent decades another form of hunger-strike is practised: that of undertaking a fast to draw attention to the sad plight of starving people in the Third World and raising funds for their relief.

The outstanding embodiment of the penitential element in Irish spirituality in the present century was a Dublin workman, Matt Talbot, the cause of whose beatification is at an advanced stage. Born in 1856, the son of a dock labourer, Matt became an alcoholic in his early teens and is reputed not to have drawn a sober breath for sixteen years. Sacrificing all to drink, he arrived home more than once in his bare feet, having pawned his shoes for drink-money. But extreme though he was in drunkenness, Matt's conversion at the age of twenty-eight was still more extreme. As one of his fellow workers put it: 'he could never go easy on anything.'[13] What that little comment meant in practice is revealed in some small way by the following account of his new life-style:

> Ten hours of every day were now spent on his knees in fervent prayer. He would rise from his plank bed at 2.00 a.m. and pray with outstretched arms till 4.00 a.m. when he prepared himself for his first Mass. If he arrived early, he would kneel outside the church in all weathers on bare knees (his trouser legs having been slit to admit the penitential cold). After hearing the maximum number of Masses, he completed his devotions with Stations of the Cross and arrived home at 7.00 a.m. for a frugal breakfast of dry bread and a mixture of cold tea and cocoa, taken without milk or sugar. His other meals varied only slightly from this meagre diet. During the last thirteen years of his life he wore penitential chains which were only revealed after his death.[14]

Matt's devotion to the Mass (he heard as many as twenty one in the space of two consecutive mornings), his love and devotion to Jesus in the Blessed Sacrament, and his recitation of the fifteen mysteries of the rosary every day, made him one of the greatest exponents of traditional spirituality the country has ever known. Nor was he lacking in good works. After he had paid off all his drinking bills of former years, his wages went entirely to the poor at home and abroad except for what he had to retain for rent and food.[15]

Before ending my remarks on the penitential aspect of Irish spirituality, I wish to add two love-letters. Daniel O'Connell, the greatest European of his day in the reckoning of many non-Irish historians, corresponded regularly, even daily for years, with his wife. Overburdened with work though he often was, be-

tween his activities at the House of Commons in London and his
work at the bar, O'Connell was strict and traditional in his observance of the Lenten fast, as the following letters from his wife
testify:

April 4th, 1816

My darling love,
For your sake I wish next week was over. I really fear you
will starve yourself. The Lent is observed so much more
strictly in Cork than here, but recollect, Darling, you ought to
take care of yourself.[16]

And again, from Dublin, on 8th April:

My dearest love,
...How happy I am to hear from Ellen Connor that your spir-
its were so good in Tralee. I am sure, darling, your fasting
and abstinence ought to have kept them down for by what I
can learn you have observed BOTH most strictly. I will venture to say there were few priests who did more...[17]

If the people of Navan, in Co Meath, saw it fitting for the priest
to dance at the Consecration of the Mass when Thady Elliot lilted
Planxty Connor, so the O'Connell couple in their love-letters did
not see anything unusual in addressing themselves to matters of
penance.

Detailed legislation governing the practice of penance has
now been superceded by an invitation to take personal responsibility for it. Pope Paul VI in *Paenitemini*[18] offers a good basis for a
modern approach to penance. In the transition from the legal to
the personal, the concept of penance as a Christian value may
get lost. This is often expressed in the phrase 'the challenge is
gone out of religion', and by 'challenge' is meant 'the penitential
element'. A person may never have heard of *Paenitemini*, much
less of its contents, but their instincts are right. In the Celtic
world, more than among other peoples perhaps, the 'challenge'

makes for a more fulfilled life and is a necessary expression of the soul's yearning for God.

But 'grace is everywhere' as Bernanos's dying Curé says, echoing St Thérèse. It is not confined to the expressly ecclesiastical events in life. Nor is it evenly effective in the life of an individual or a community. My friend Gerry may be careless as to sacramental practice, but there is pure grace in his scrupulous observance of Lenten self-denial. Michael and Maeve may, much of the time, be busily engaged in trying to earn a living and raise their large family, but what a deep well of gracious hospitality must be in them that leads them to bring home a group of chance-met foreign tourists and treat them to an afternoon of food and song and dance before putting them on the train for the next leg of their tour. The old Fenian at the turn of the century may not have attended Mass or had anything to do with the official church since his excommunication more than thirty five years previously, but every day he said two rosaries 'that the Irish bishops will see the light.' Christy, deprived and handicapped in a poor part of Dublin, loses himself in the first painful journey to calvary and embodies its grace in a poem, *Good Friday*:

> In and out among the narrow little ways of the town
> They dragged Him, bearded Man, and the
> gems of sweat
> On His brow glittered like gold-dust
> In the merciless fire of noon-day.
> Sticks flashed and thudded dully on straining flesh;
> Taunts, maledictions, words sharp
> with scorn and hate,
> Sank as fire into the tired brain;
>
> Spits bright with foulness ran as lava
> down His chest,
> And the cruel, thin stones of the hillside
> Made the blood run from the stumbling Feet,
> Staining the earth with a crimson glory.

On they dragged Him, the cross's shadow on His back,
Up the awaiting hill, as an animal to the slaughter-house.
He gazed forlorn, with timeless pity
upon the deriding multitude.

Sunk in the agony of betrayal, His denied majesty
A crown of thorns girding the tranquil brown;
And there, Fatherless, they nailed Him to a
beam of mountain wood,

And the pain-bright eyes gazed into the deeps
of all that had been
and was yet to be,

Surveying His world, His desecrated Garden, hanging
from the cross
Upon a brooding hill, a bleeding Ecstasy.[19]

When the church is seen as institution only it is difficult for people on the margins who are more attuned to the traditional faith-ways to maintain comfortable links with it. Too often church membership and practice is reduced to being 'all in' or 'all out.' The criterion for belonging is narrowed down to only one element of the many splendoured Christian tradition. At her wise and confident best the church has always been relaxed and generous about her boundaries. Many belong to God, Augustine said, who do not belong (formally) to the church; and many belong to the church who do not belong to God. Fellow travellers have always been welcome on the pilgrimage of life.

In defensive or disorganised times, however, a certain tightening-up may be called for. Such was the case in later eighteenth and nineteenth century Ireland. Re-ordering was necessary and the institutional side of church life came to the fore. This always brings its dangers.

The Catholic philosopher and spiritual writer, Baron Frederick Von Hugel (1852-1925), distinguishes three elements in church life: the mystical, the intellectual and the institutional. If any one of these becomes dominant, if all three are not held in dynamic balance, each complementing and nourishing the others, the overall wellbeing suffers. In nineteenth century Ireland the institutional element needed building up, but in the process the native Irish mystical element suffered serious eclipse and the intellectual element was not allowed room to develop freely. Many tensions in late twentieth-century Irish Catholicism are rooted in this imbalance, as we shall explore in our final chapter.

CHAPTER 6

Parting Thoughts

That wonderful catechist, the late Christianne Brusselmans, once told me that the Irish she met on the continent had faith but were appallingly ignorant of their religion. Those whom she instructed were often at first meeting both hostile and resistant but later became 'apostles.' The journey from hostility to apostleship was an interesting one.

Christianne dealt with parents who wished to have their children suitably instructed in preparation for the celebration of the Sacraments of Initiation namely, Baptism, Confirmation and first Holy Communion. Being a thoroughly conscientious woman, she required the parents of these children to attend nine catechetical sessions over the months prior to the date set for the sacrament. She would not allow any child to go forward for a sacrament unless both parents had attended these two-to-three-hour sessions because she wanted the parents to be thoroughly aware of the meaning and implications of that for which they were putting their child forward.

Christianne's first experience of many Irish parents was that they wanted to get as far away from the Catholic Church as they possibly could. At the same time, illogically, they were anxious to ensure that their children not only got all the benefits of secular education but also got initiated into the reality that they still intuitively knew to be of profound importance, even though their own adult practice was sporadic and superficial.

Reluctant to be drawn into further involvement themselves, they would say to Christianne that they were too busy to attend her sessions: a grind in French on Monday, Badminton on

Tuesday, Swimming on Wednesday – each day had its own prior commitment. And to this litany Christianne would gently reply: 'Ah you are very *boozy* (her Flemish pronunciation of 'busy': not a reference to our drinking habits). Maybe next year you will not be so *boozy*, or maybe the year after.' And so the interview would end.

The sequel was always interesting. It might take the form of an awkward phonecall, virtually always made by the woman. She would say that herself and her husband were having a second look at their busy schedule and that they might after all be able to fit in those sessions. To this Christianne would reply, *'Gooth!'* Then, with some fumbling for words the caller would anxiously ask if attending these lectures would mean having to go to Confession or Communion. 'Oh, no,' Christianne would reply, 'I just want to be sure that you are both properly aware of that to which you are committing your child.'

In due time the course would begin. Yes, an initial reluctance, even hostility, a sense of coercion perhaps, but beneath it all a dormant faith. Evening by evening, as Christianne nourished the intellect, that faith began to awaken, revive, grow strong and ultimately blossom. Almost invariably these couples didn't just re-discover the faith of their childhood, but began to enjoy a new intellectually satisfying experience of the Christian reality in all its richness and variety, so well communicated by the saintly Christianne. In the end they would come forward to express their thanks to her saying: 'For the first time in our lives we *understand* our Catholic faith.' And from that new understanding and the joy of having found 'the pearl of great price', their life took on something of the excitement of the apostles in the first days of Pentecost.

The intellectual side of the Irish church is still in crisis. It is probably safe to say that most of the leaders and image makers and trend setters in Ireland today have no adult intellectual grasp of their faith and possess little more than memories of instruction for first Holy Communion. How sad that so many of these people presume to pronounce publicly on church matters, and even on theological topics, out of such childish knowledge. Would they venture to pontificate similarly about science, say, or economics, or farming, without doing adult homework. Helen Waddell was right: 'We tolerate cheap thinking in ourselves about religion, as we tolerate it about nothing else.'[1]

Because there is no theology faculty in most of our universities, the vast majority of our Catholic students who might wish to get an adult grasp of their faith have no opportunity of pursuing such knowledge at third level. It may be asked if the institution's concern for control of theological thinking is not a root cause of intellectual malnutrition among Irish Catholics and of 'the plodding blandness of Irish theology,' (to quote a friend). It may also account at least in part for the bitter hunger of Austin Clarke and many like him who were intuitively aware of the narrowness and poverty of Irish Catholicism as they had experienced it, but hadn't the intellectual formation and development to cope with it or rise above the ecclesiastical pettiness.

In Ireland today, the institutional church has largely lost its political clout, but the heavy hand of institution still (fearfully now) tries to hold on to control within the Catholic ranks, and theological watchdogs still thrive. For two or three decades past some efforts are being made to deal with the problem of ignorance of the faith, but the absence of theology in the universities still screams out for urgent attention.

The present rude 'sweeping of things off the dresser' is rooted in the intellectual poverty of 'Catholicism of the Irish kind'. In public life it results in the empty secularisation of rich traditional Christian feasts. St Patrick's Day has been hijacked by commerce and is reduced increasingly in public utterance to 'Paddy's Day' – an accurate enough term in view of the commercial parades and capers with which it is 'celebrated'!

A friend of mine spent the recent St Patrick's Day in Ottawa. He wrote in a letter: 'The Mass was due to start at 10.30 am but the Basilica was full at 10 am. They were a most attentive group and there was a great sense of reverence. Later when I looked at the news it seemed so hollow to have dyed the Liffey green and to see a parade that was more suitable to Brazil at carnival time.'

In a similar secularist evacuation of ancient church feasts, All Saints' and Pentecost have been supplanted by bank holidays in October and June respectively – in the middle of nowhere, adrift from all tradition. (The conjunction of bank and 'holy-day' goes unnoticed but all too accurately expresses the transfer of allegiance from God to mammon.) By contrast, France, despite the Revolution, is still publicly respectful of the Christian ethos. It observes public holidays on the feasts of the Ascension of Our Lord, the Assumption of Our Lady and All Saints; and even in Paris the commercial world (including corner shops) closes down from early afternoon on Holy Thursday until late afternoon on Good Friday, while at New Year the local newsagents expressly advertise their calendars for the year ahead as 'having all the feasts.' There is a growing trend in Irish calendars not to mention even Easter Sunday.

As well as having a *catholicisme du type irlandais*, we seem to have a *secularisme du type irlandais* as well: it is bitter and vengeful, anti-church and anti-clerical and constantly revisiting the old spiritual home in order to smash more delph! While it is capable of raising its head at any time of year, it is much in evidence around St Patrick's Day when we frequently hear pronouncements to the effect that Ireland might be far better off had the National Apostle and Christianity never reached our shores. The purveyors of such notions are selective and unreal in picturing a pagan past where everybody was liberated, fulfilled and happy. Their main nostalgia seems to be an adolescent dream of uninhibited sexual freedom. In such flights of fancy they forget that every society needs its moral enclosures in order to survive. And they conveniently ignore the fact that the predominant characteristic in all pagan religion is fear; fear that anxiously and obsequiously struggles to placate and manipulate the capricious and unreliable powers.

Much of this adolescent 'post-catholic' floundering is a reaction to the excessive institutionalisation from which the Irish church, and the church at large, is now emerging. The institutional, while essential to the church, does have an inherent ten-

dency to take over the whole life of the faithful and to devour all
else. This would seem to be a recurring pattern in church history.

The supreme age of institutionalisation dates roughly from
the time of Pope Pius IX to that of Pius XII (c. 1850-1950), and
that coincides exactly with the modern reorganisation and institutionalisation of the church in Ireland.

Typical of institutional religion is the focusing of attention on
the person in authority: he is seen or proclaimed as the bearer of
truth, the guide, the one to be obeyed. There is also considerable
stress on structure, hierarchy, law and discipline. The priest and
the bishop loom large as authority figures and command great
loyalty and equally great opposition. But this opposition is not
to themselves as persons – there has never been a shortage of
that – but opposition to the institution. When there is far more
talk about the bishops than about the faith and Christ and Mary,
then the institution has asserted itself over the tradition.

Such an approach is ultimately to the detriment of genuine
religious tradition and the consequences become obvious: a decline in the general popular transmission of the faith and of
prayer. It becomes more and more the work of the institution to
take responsibility for these things. There is less and less room
for the person of genuine tradition who could and did respect
the institution, but never identified with it or saw it as more than
the servant of faith and life.

In the institutionalisation process, the people hand over to
that institution ever greater responsibility for the maintenance
and transmission of their faith. Church ruling replaces in large
part the personal and conscience aspects of the faith. This results
in a 'culture of dependency' among the faithful. Inevitably a reaction against this sets in, a healthy and proper self-assertion.
Most people negotiate this phase quietly and sensibly enough;
some seem to need to do it more publicly, and often shrilly and
bitterly.

Interestingly, such cries and protests often centre on sexual
morality. Part of the blanket institutionalisation in the church
was a heavy-handed moralism and legalism about human be-

haviour. Some theologians and analysts would now suggest that much atheism and indifference today (not just in Ireland) is the direct result of the excessive preoccupation of the church with morals over the last century or two. Many lively and thoughtful people felt the church's moral teaching as stifling rather than guiding their lives. It's an intriguing thought that current looseness and excess in sexual behaviour and discussion may be the *sensus fidelium* reasserting itself again!

In the long run, the over-dominant institution devours the very thing on which it depends and feeds, namely, the personal and communal faith and commitment of the people. In the final analysis, one is left with big churches, big plans, streamlined organisations, and nobody there. This process has already worked itself through in much of Continental Europe and the same painful process is presently going on in Ireland.

We may schematise the process or cycle as follows:

1) The Good News is preached.
2) There is a faith-response from the people.
3) The institution emerges and builds on it.
4) The institution devours the popular faith.
5) The faith weakens.
6) The institution collapses.
7) The Good News is preached anew.

In *The Gems She Wore*, James Plunkett wrote 'The Church had excommunicated the Fenians, it had condemned practically everything I later came to regard as worthwhile, yet for mature men of my childhood, even those who had suffered grievously from its intolerance, it guarded a Truth which was better than the sum of all its wrongheadedness.'[2] There are signs that mature men and women of our own time are coming to the same realisation. From the present uncertainty a more robust faith will surely emerge – how widely held, no one can yet say. But neither can anyone say that the apparent trend towards indifference and secularisation will continue inexorably. (The Anglican Dean Inge [1860-1954] said that 'Those who wed the spirit of the age

must expect to find themselves widowed in a very short time!')
Who can reckon with the depths of the Irish soul, not to mention
the grace of the great God of Our Lord Jesus Christ?

There is a Zen saying which runs: 'When my house burned
down, I got an unobstructed view of the moon at night.' Perhaps
our present church structures, cluttered and obstructive as
many still find them, will have to crumble further before the face
of Christ can be seen clearly and joyously again. Somehow that
beloved face seems to be indelibly engraved on the Irish soul.
Racial and religious characteristics known to have existed for a
millennium or two, are still with us; and as the anthropologist
Marret said: 'Survivals are no mere wreckage of the past, but are
likewise symptomatic of those tendencies of our common nature
which have the best chance of survival in the long run.'[3]

What the future holds is unknown. But fifteen hundred years
of history cannot be unwritten or forgotten. Nor can the deeply
scored lines and scars of Christian religiousness (incorporating
the pre-Christian) be easily erased from the Irish soul.

In a book review in the *Catholic Herald*, Donal Giltinan some
twenty seven years ago said: 'I remember an occasion when I
was sitting, as a young man, with Seán Ó Faoláin and the late
Maurice Walsh. Something brash that I had said made Maurice
inquire of Ó Faoláin: 'Is he a Catholic?' 'He's not now,' said
Seán, with considerable insight. 'But he'll die one.'

Notes

INTRODUCTION

1. De Paor, *St Patrick's World*, p. 3.
2. Gallagher, M.P., *The Furrow*, (25) 1974, p. 185.
3. Kavanagh, P., *The Complete Poems*, p. 84.
4. Arensberg, C., *The Irish Countryman*, quoted on p. 181.
5. Kavanagh, P., op. cit., p. 160.
6. From the oral Tradition in Kiskeam, Co Cork.
7. Hyde, D., *The Religious Songs of Connaught*, (ii) p. 23.

CHAPTER ONE
(THE 'CELTIC CHURCH')

1. Paul VI, *Evangelii Nuntiandi*, 8-12-1975, passim; M.P. Gallagher's *Clashing Symbols*, pp. 52-53; 101-102.
2. Brown, Ed., *Poetry of Irish History*, pp. 3-5.
3. MacCana, P, *Celtic Mythology*, p. 11.
4. ibid., pp. 12, 14.
5. vide: Sigerson, G., *Bards of the Gael and Gall*, Pref. to 2nd ed., p.1.
6. Meyer, Kuno, *Selection from Ancient Irish Poetry*, p. vii.
7. ibid., p. ix.
8. De Paor, L., *St Patrick's World*, p. 7.
9. Duffy, J., *Patrick in his own words*, passim.
10. Renan, E., *Poetry of the Celtic Races and Other Stories*, quoted in A. Carmichael's *Carmina Gadelica*, (i) p. xxxiii.
11. Carmichael, A., *Carmina Gadelica*, (i) p. xxxiii.
12. Two of Patrick's writings survive, namely, the *Confession of Grace* (alias, 'The Confession') and the *Letter excommunicating Coroticus* (alias, 'The Letter to Coroticus').
13. De Paor, L, *St Patrick's World*, p. 6.
14. Conneely, D., *The Letters of St Patrick*, p. 109.
15. ibid. p. 214.
16. ibid., pp. 13, 161, passim.
17. Duffy, J., *Patrick in his own words*, p. 18.
18. ibid., pp. 33-34.
19. Herren, M., in *Sages, Saints and Storytellers* , (ed. D. Ó Corráin) p. 77.

20. ibid.
21. vide: De Paor, L., *St Patrick's World*, pp. 46 sq.
22. vide: Ó Fiaich, T., in *CIH* , p. 65.
23. ibid., p. 67.
24. An ancient tradition attests that when St Mel was receiving Brigid's vows, he inadvertently read the text for the ordination of a bishop. When this was brought to his notice he said: let it be!
25. O'Curry, E., *Manners and Customs of the Ancient Irish* , (i) p. lxxix.
26. Murphy, G. & Knott E., *Early Irish Literature*, p. xii.
27. Ginnell, L. *The Brehon Laws*, p. 3.
28. ibid., pp. 5-6. Alfred the Great, King of England at end of 9th century is said to have been educated in Ireland.
29. O'Curry, E., op. cit., (ii) p. 73.
30. ibid., p. 74.
31. O'Rahilly, C. (ed) 'Táin Bó Cúalnge,' in *ITS*, (49), p. 272.
32. *ZCP*, 9, p. 470; trs. Francis Mullaghy, CSSR.
33. *Book of Hy Many*, 119a; trs. Francis Mullaghy, CSSR.
34. Trs. Francis Mullaghy, CSSR.
35. Green, D., 'Early Irish Society' in *Early Irish Society*, M. Dillon, (ed), p. 87.
36. Macquarrie, J., *Pathways in Spirituality*, p. 123.
37. O'Curry, E., op. cit., (ii) p. 75.
38. Healy, J, *The Life and Writings of St Patrick*, pp. 707-708.
39. Kennelly, B., *A Drinking Cup*, p. 17.
40. Tr. Kuno Meyer, in *Ériu*, (i), 1904, p. 40.
41. Keating, G., *The History of Ireland*, P. S. Dinneen, (ed), *ITS*, (9) iii, p. 7341.
42. Stokes,W. & Strachan, J., *Thesaurus Palaeohibernicus*, (ii) p. 327.
43. Meyer, K., *Selections from Ancient Irish Poetry*, pp. xii-xiii.
44. vide: McNally, R., *Old Ireland*, p. 37.
45. Carney, J., 'The Poems of Blathmac Son of Cú Brettan' in *ITS* (xlvii) 1964, pp. 3-49, passim.
46. Murphy, G., *Early Irish Lyrics*, p. 33.
47. vide: ibid., pp. 33-35.
48. Tr. Kuno Meyer, in *Ériu*, (vi), p. 112.
49. Tr. Francis Mullaghy, CSSR.
50. Gougaud, L., quoted in 'Irish Spirituality in Antiquity' by F. Cayré in *The Miracle of Ireland*, (ed) Daniel-Rops, p. 110.
51. Kennelly, B., *A Drinking Cup*, p. 21.
52. vide: O'Curry, E., op. cit., (ii) pp. 69-70.
53. Kennelly, B., op. cit., (ii) p. 19.
54. vide: McNally, R., *Old Ireland*, p. 41.
55. ibid. p. 47.
56. Duffy, J., *Patrick in his own words*, pp. 30-31.
57. Ó Fiaich, T., in *CIH*, p. 68.
58. Walker, G. S. M., *Sancti Columbani Opera*, p. 122.

59. vide: Ryan, J., *Irish Monasticism*, pp. 334-335; and ft. nt. 1, p. 335.
60. vide: Stokes, W., *Féilire Oengusso Céilí Dé*, p. xcviii; Tr. Flower, R., *The Irish Tradition*, p. 53.
61. Kennelly, B., *A Drinking Cup*, p. 15.
62. From the *Leabhar Breac*, p. 262b; Tr. K. Meyer in *Ériu*, (3) pp. 15 sq.
63. Ryan, J., *Irish Monasticism*, p. 347 sq.
64. ibid., 349.
65. Edmonds, D.C., *The Early Scottish Church*, p. 264.
66. ibid.
67. ibid., 67.
68. O'Curry, E., op. cit., (ii) p. 74.
69. Edmonds, D. C., op. cit., p. 274.
70. Stokes,W., *Féilire Oengusso Céilí Dé*, p. xlix.
71. Ryan, J., op. cit., p. 348
72. Stokes,W., op. cit., p. xlix.
73. ibid., passim.
74. Hennesy, W.M., *Annals of Loch Cé*, p. 103.
75. Edmonds, D. C., op. cit., p. 281.
76. Stokes, W., *Lives of the Saints from the Book of Lismore*, p. 259.
77. Stokes,W., *Féilire Oengusso Céilí Dé*, p. xlviii.
78. ibid., p. 56.
79. Curtayne, A., *The Irish Story*, pp. 34-35.
80. ibid., p. 35.
81. Rolleston, T.W., *A Treasury of Irish Poetry*, p. 460.
82. vide: Hanson, W. G., *The Early Monastic Schools of Ireland*, p. 2.
83. Bede, St, *History of the English Church and People*, iii, 27. In the mid 1970s while studying in a programme known as Seattle University Masters of Religious Education (SUMORE), I composed a quatrain giving my response to Bede's remarks on Irish generosity:
   In SUMORE I have no such thrills
   For all things here cost dollar bills;
   O happy would I be indeed
   Could I but say the same as Bede.
84. Montalambert, C., *The Monks of the West from St Benedict to St Bernard* (ii) p. 126.
85. vide: Traube, quoted in *The Irish*, by Seán Ó Faolain, p. 50.
86. Curtayne, A., *The Irish Story*, p. 26.
87. MacManus, S., *The Story of the Irish Race*, p. 215.
88. Walker, G. S., *Sancti Columbani Opera*, p. 49; and vide: p. 47.
89. Edmonds, D. C., op. cit., p. 281.
90. MacCarthy, Daniel, *Life of St Columba translated from the Latin of St Adamnán*, (Dublin) n.d. p. 5.
91. This is P. H. Pearse's translation of Seathrún Céitin's poem *Mo bheannacht leat, a sgríbhinn*.
92. Stokes, W., *Lives of the Saints from the Book of Lismore*, pp. 169-170.
93. Strabo, W., *Vita S. Galli* II, 46, quoted by G. Murphy in *Studies*, (17) 65, 1928, p. 41

94. Péronne had such a strong Irish connection during the early-middle-ages that it was known as 'Péronne of the Irish.'

95. O'Donovan, J., *The Ancient Irish Church*, p. 55.

96. Stokes, W. & Strachan, J., *Thesaurus Palaeohibernicus*, (ii) p. 296; Tr. John J. Ó Ríordáin, CSSR.

97. Plummer, C., *Vitae Sanctorum Hiberniae*, (ii) p. 260. Tr. Gerald Crotty, CSSR.

98. Murphy, G., in *Studies* (17) 66, 1928, p. 230.

99. ibid., (65) p. 47.

100. ibid., (66) p. 246.

101. ibid., p. 242.

102. T. Ó Fiaich, *Gaelscrínte san Eoraip*, p. 22.

103. Zimmer, H, *The Irish Element in Mediaeval Culture*, quoted in MacManus, S., *The Story of the Irish Race*, p. 212-213.

104. MacCana, P., *Celtic Mythology*, p. 131-132.

105. Sigerson, G., *Bards of the Gael and Gall*, pp. 207-208.

CHAPTER TWO

(THE LATE MEDIAEVAL PERIOD)

1. Stokes, W., *Féilire Oengusso Céilí Dé*, p. 210.

2. Murphy, G., *Early Irish Lyrics*, p. 71.

3. Ó Cuív, B., *Seven Centuries of Irish Learning*, passim.

4. Hennessy, W. M. (ed), *Annals of Loch Cé*, (ii) p. 127.

5. St Bernard, *Life of Malachy*, tr. Dean Lawlor; quoted by A. Gwynn SJ in *IER* (71) 1949, p. 142.

6. ibid. p. 143.

7. ibid.

8. Ó Cuív, B., op. cit., pp. 14-15.

9. ibid., p. 15.

10. vide: Curtis, E., *Calendar of Ormond Deeds*, (ii) p. 168; Carney, J., *Mediaeval Irish Lyrics*, p. 100.

11. ibid. p. 169.

12. Fitzmaurice, E.B. & Little, A.G., *Materials for the History of the Franciscan Province of Ireland*, p. 157.

13. MacNeill, E., *Early Irish Laws and Institutions*, pp. 145-47.

14. Healy, J., *The Life and Writings of St Patrick*, pp. 661-662.

15. ibid., p. 659.

16. ibid., p. 664.

17. ibid., p. 658.

18. Knott, E., (ed. & tr.) *The Poems of Tadhg Dall Ó Huiginn*, ITS (23), p. 290.

19. ibid., pp. 291-292

20. Dillon, M., *Early Irish Literature*, p. 101.

21. ibid., p. 37.

22. Knott, E., *Irish Classical Poetry*, p. 77.

23. ibid., pp. 77-78.

24. Knott, E., *Irish Classical Poetry* (1960 ed.), p. 80.

25. Mooney, C., in *HIC* (ii) 5, p. 42.

26. O'Dwyer, P., *Towards a History of Irish Spirituality*, p. 118.

27. McKenna, L., (ed), *Dánta Dé*, p. 49; (Tr.) quoted by Mooney, op. cit.,
    p. 40, ft. n. 33.

28. Bergin, O., *Irish Bardic Poetry*, p. 302.

29. McKenna, L. (ed), *Dánta Aonghus Fionn Ó Dálaigh*, pp.viii-xiii, pas-
    sim.

30. Bergin, O., op. cit., p. 302.

31. ibid., p. 301-302.

32. Knott, E., (ed. & tr.), *The Poems of Tadhg Dall Ó Huiginn*, *ITS* (23), p.
    145.

33. ibid., p. 159.

34. Ó Floinn, D., *The Integral Irish Tradition*, pp. 11-12, with minor textual
    alterations in the translation.

35. ibid., p. 9.

36. ibid.

37. Quoted by D. Ó Laoghaire in *Irish Spirituality*, p. 5.

38. Ó Laoghaire, D., *Irish Spirituality*, p. 12.

39. ibid.

40. Mooney, C., *HIC* (ii) 5, *The Church in Gaelic Ireland*, p. 56.

41. ibid.

42. ibid.

43. ibid., p. 59.

44. ibid., p. 57.

45. Mooney, C., in *IER* (99) 1963, p106.

46. Mooney, C., *HIC* (ii) 5, p. 18.

47. ibid.

48. ibid., p. 20.

49. ibid., p. 61.

50. Ó Laoghaire, D., *Irish Spirituality*, pp. 8-9.

51. ibid., p. 10.

52. Mooney, C., in *IER* (99) 1963, pp. 104-105.

55. ibid., p. 102.

56. Mangan, J. C., *Poems of James Clarence Mangan*, pp. 3-5.

CHAPTER THREE

('IRISH AND CATHOLIC')

1. Mooney, C., *IER* (99) 1963, p. 107.

2. A stock phrase in the ancient Annals, e.g. The *Annals of Loch Cé*,
   under the year AD 1118 reads: Dermot Ua Briain, king of Mumha,

and of all Leth-Mogha, died at Corcachmor of Mumha, after unction and penance.'

3. Mooney, op. cit. p. 103.
4. Tr. John J., Ó Ríordáin CSSR; for original Latin, see *IER* (69) 1947, p. 136.
5. vide: Eamon Duffy's 'The Reformation Revisited' in *The Tablet*, March 4th 1995.
6. Hayes-McCoy, G.A., in *CIH*, p. 181.
7. McLysaght, E., *Irish Life in the Seventeenth Century*, p. 286.
8. *State Papers*, Henry VIII, vol. ii (b), p. 141.
9. O'Halloran, S., *History of Ireland* (ii) p. 210-211.
10. ibid., p. 212.
11. McLysaght, op. cit., p. 284.
12. vide: ibid., p. 284.
13. vide: ibid, pp. 284-285 and ft. nt. 7a.
14. Corish, P.J., in *HIC* (iii) 8, p. 30.
15. Curtayne, A., *The Irish Story*, p. 92.
16. Clarke, A., in *CIH*, p. 202.
17. Curtayne, op. cit., p. 104.
18. Millett, Benignus, OFM, in *HIC* (iii), 7, p. 2.
19. Carlyle, T., *Cromwell's Letters and Speeches*, (ii) p. 86.
20. *Cambrensis Eversus*, Gratianus Lucius Hibernus (1662) Dublin 1848, pp. 72-73, ft. nt. h.
21. Curtayne, op. cit. p. 93-94.
22. Clarke, A., *The Old English in Ireland*, 1625-42, pp. 10-11.
23. Hayes, R., *Old Irish Links with France*, p. 19, ft. nt. 2.
24. ibid.
25. MacErlain, *Poems of David Ó Bruadair*, in *ITS* (18) p. 15.
26. Lecky, quoted by P. Colum in *The Road Round Ireland*, p. 436.
27. Corish, P. J., *The Catholic Community in the 17th & 18th Century*, p. 72.
28. ibid.
29. ibid., p. 73.
30. Curtayne, op. cit., p. 108-109.
31. Lecky, W., quoted in *HIC* (iv) 2, p. 2.
32. McLysaght, op. cit., p. 280-281.
33. Corkery, D., *The Hidden Ireland*, p. 265.
34. vide: Curtayne, *The Irish Story*, p. 110.
35. ibid., p. 107.
36. Brady, J. in *HIC* (iv) 2, p. 5.
37. Young, A., *Arthur Young's Tour of Ireland*, (ii) part II, p. 44.
38. Ó Laoghaire, D., *Ár bPaidreacha Dúchais*, pp. 25-48.
39. Ó Laoghaire, D., *Our Mass Our Life*, p. 8.
40. ibid.
41. ibid.
42. ibid., p. 11.
43. ibid., p. 12.
44. ibid., pp. 16-17.

45. ibid., p. 17, ft. nt.1.
46. The more notable collections include:
    Ár bPaidreacha Dúchais, D. Ó Laoghaire, SJ;
    Paidreacha na nDaoine, Searlóid Ní Dhéisighe;
    Prayers of the Gael, R. MacCrócaigh (a translation of *Paidreacha na nDaoine*);
    Religious Songs of Connaught, Douglas Hyde;
    Urnaigh na nGael, An tAthair Uinseann, OCSC;
    Our Mass our Life, D. Ó Laoghaire SJ;
    Amhra Coimrí, An tAthair Seán Ó Duinn, OSB;
47. Ó Laoghaire, *Our Mass Our Life*, p. 27.
48. ibid., p. 24.
49. ibid., pp. 28-29.
50. ibid., p. 36.
51. Madgett, Nicholas, *Constitutio Ecclesiastica*, (i), pp. 132-133.
52. Brady, J., in *IER* (70) 1948, p. 516.
53. Power, P. Canon, *A Bishop in the Penal Times*, p. 18.
54. ibid., p. 22.
55. ibid., p. 34.
56. Ó Laoghaire, *Irish Spirituality*, pp. 9-10.
57. Mould, D. D. C Pochin, *Irish Pilgrimage*, p. 29.
58. ibid.
59. Madgett, op. cit., (ii) p. 416.
60. MacCrócaigh, R., *Prayers of the Gael*, p. 56.
61. Hyde, D., *Religious Songs of Connaught*, (ii) pp. 6-9.
62. MacCrócaigh, op. cit., p. 59.
63. ibid., p. 57.
64. O'Sullivan, D., *Carolan*, (ii), p. 146.
65. Carmichael, A., *Carmina Gadelica*, (i) p. xxxiii.
66. Hayes, op. cit., p. 13.

CHAPTER FOUR

('CATHOLICISM OF THE IRISH KIND')

1. vide: Fennell, D., *The Changing Face of Catholic Ireland*, p. 13.
2. ibid.
3. Smyth, SJ, K., *The Furrow* (9) 1958, p. 137.
4. Brady, J., in *IER* (70) 1948, pp. 520-521.
5. ibid., p. 521.
6. ibid.
7. ibid.
8. Fennell, D., op. cit., p. 15.
9. ibid., p. 37.
10. *Annals of Ulster*, pp. 428, 430.
11. Madgett, N., *Constitutio Ecclesiasticae*, (ii) p. 370.
12. vide: 'Marriage and population growth in Ireland 1750-1845,' in

Economic History Review, series ii, xvi, 1963, pp. 301-13; also *Ireland since the Famine,* by F.S.L. Lyons, Glasgow, 1974, pp. 39-41 and footnotes passim; MacLysaght, E., *Irish Life in the Seventeen Century,* p. 47, 'Marriage in its full sense was common at seventeen or eighteen.'

13. Fennell, D., op. cit., p. 41.
14. Corish, P., *The Catholic Community in the 17th & 18th Century,* p. 87.
15. De Bhál, T., in *Studies in Pastoral Liturgy* (3), pp. 211-214.
16. Corish, P., *The Irish Catholic Experience,* p. 131.
17. vide: ibid., p. 114.
18. De Bhál, T., op. cit., p. 214.
19. Fennell, D., op. cit., p. 37.
20. vide: *The Freeman's Journal,* 23-8, 1850; P.C. Barry in *ITQ* (26), p. 134.
21. Barry, P. C., in *ITQ* (26), p. 136.
22. Larkin, E., in *AHR* (77) 1972, p. 638.
23. Cannon, CSSR, S., *Irish Episcopal Meetings, 1788-1882,* p. 127.
24. ibid., p. 127-28.
25. Barry, P. C., in *ITQ* (26) 1959, p. 132.
26. McSuibhne, P., *Paul Cullen and his Contemporaries* (i), p. 331.
27. Larkin, E., op. cit., p. 648.
28. Moriarty, Rt Rev Dr, *Allocutions to the clergy & Pastorals,* p. 64.
29. ibid., p. 56.
30. Larkin, E., op. cit., p. 635.
31. ibid., p. 636.
32. ibid.
33. Barry, P. C., *ITQ* (26) 1959, p. 140 sq.
34. ibid., p. 141.
35. ibid.
36. Larkin, E., op. cit., p. 636.
37. Barry, P. C., *ITQ* (26) 1959, p. 140.
38. Wakeman, W.F., *Three Days on the Shannon,* pp. 30-31.
39. Larkin, E., op. cit., p. 637.
40. Corish, P., *The Irish Catholic Experience,* p. 171.
41. Larkin, E., op. cit., p. 638.
42. ibid.
43. ibid., p. 646.
44. Dating roughly from Cullen's arrival in Ireland in 1850.
45. Ó hÁinle, C., in *The Furrow* (27) 1976, p. 583.
46. Clarke, A., *Poems,* 1955-66, p. 203.

CHAPTER FIVE

('FASTING LIKE AN IRISHMAN')

1. Chinnéide, S. Ní, *Kerry Archaeological Journal* (6) 1973, pp. 83-100.
2. ibid., p. 98.
3. ibid.

4. ibid., pp. 98-99.
5. Fenton, S., *It All Happened*, p. 30.
6. vide: Hutton, A.W., (ed.) *Arthur Young's Tour in Ireland* (ii), pp. 146-47.
7. ibid., p. 47.
8. Danagher, K., *The Year in Ireland*, p. 228.
9. Carbery, M., *The Farm by Lough Gur*, p. 204.
10. Walsh, M., *Knock: The Shrine of the Pilgrim People of God*, pp. 103-104.
11. The term 'rounds' is a reference to walking *deiseal* (right-handedly, clock-wise or sun-wise) around the well or holy place, while at the same time reciting certain prayers – usually Paters, Aves and Glorias, or perhaps the entire rosary. It is a curious feature of the rounds at Knock that most people walk *tuathail* (anti-clockwise) the traditional Irish Celtic motion for cursing!
12. MacNeill, M., *The Festival of Lughnasa*, passim.
13. Johnston, F., *Adict for Christ*, p. 5.
14. ibid., p. 8.
15. Purcell, M., *The Making of Matt Talbot*, pp. 18-27 passim.
16. O'Connell, M. R., *The Correspondence of Daniel O'Connell* (ii), p. 95.
17. ibid., p. 97.
18. Pope Paul VI, *Paenetimini (Penitence)*, Catholic Truth Society, London, 1966.
19. Browne, C., *Background Music*, p. 7.

CHAPTER SIX

PARTING THOUGHTS

1. Corrigan, D. F., *Helen Waddell*, p. 188.
2. Plunkett, J., *The Gems She Wore*, p. 25.
3. Quoted in Arensberg, C., *The Irish Countryman*, p. 181.

Bibliography

Arensberg, C., *The Irish Countryman*, Clouster, Mass: Smith, 1959.

Bede, Venerable, *Ecclesiastical History and Anglo-Saxon Chronicle*, (ed.) J.A. Giles, London: Bell, 1884.

– *History of the English Church and People:* Middlesex: Penguin, 1983.

Barrington, T. J., *Discovering Kerry*, Dublin: Blackwater Press, 1976.

Behan, B., *Borstal Boy*, London: Methuen, 1975.

Bergin, O. J., *Irish Bardic Poetry*, Dublin: Inst. for Adv. Studies, 1970.

Brown, C., *Background Music – poems*, New York: Stein & Day, 1973.

Canon, S.P., *Irish Episcopal Meetings, 1788-1882*, Rome, 1976.

Carbery, M., *The Farm by Lough Gur*, Cork: Mercier, 1973.

Carlyle, Thomas, *Oliver Cromwell's Letters and Speeches* (5 vols.), London: Chapman and Hall, 1871.

Carmichael, A., *Carmina Gadelica*, 6 vols, Edinburgh: Norman Maclean, 1928.

Carney, J., *Early Irish Poetry*, Cork: Mercier, 1969.

– *Mediaeval Irish Lyrics*, Dublin: Dolmen, 1967.

Clarke, A., *The Old English in Ireland, 1625-42*, MacGibbon & Key, 1966.

Colum, P., *The Road Round Ireland*, New York: Macmillan, 1927.

Conneely, D., *St Patrick's Letters*, Maynooth: An Sagart, 1993.

Corkery, D., *The Hidden Ireland*, Dublin: Gill Paperback, 1967.

Corish, P. J., (gen. ed.) *A History of Irish Catholicism*, 6 vols, Dublin: Gill & Macmillan, 1985.

– *The Irish Catholic Experience*, Dublin: Gill, 1985.

– *The Catholic Community in the 17th & 18th Century*, Dublin: Helicon, 1981.

Corrigan, D. F., *Helen Waddell*, London: Gollancz, 1986.

Curtis, E., *A Calendar of Ormond Deeds*, 6 vols., Dublin: Stationery Office, 1932-71.

Curtayne, A., *The Irish Story*, Dublin: Clonmore & Reynolds, 1962.

Clarke, A., *Poems, 1955-66*, L. Miller (ed.), Dublin: Dolmen, 1974.

Daniel-Rops, H., (ed.) *The Miracle of Ireland*, Dublin: Clonmore & Reynolds, 1959.

Danagher, K., *The Year in Ireland*, Cork: Mercier, 1973.

DePaor, Liam, *Ireland and Early Europe*, Dublin: Four Courts Press, 1997.

– *St Patrick's World*, Dublin: Four Courts Press, 1996.

DePaor, Máire & Liam, *Early Christian Ireland*, Thames & Hudson, 1978.

Ní Dhéisighe, S., *Paidreacha na nDaoine*, Dublin, 1924.

Dillon, M., *Early Irish Literature*, Chicago & London: University Press, 1948.

– *Early Irish Society*, Cork: Mercier, 1969.

Duffy, J., *Patrick In His Own Words*, Dublin: Veritas, 1975.

Fennell, D. (ed.) *The Changing Face of Catholic Ireland*, Dublin: Chapman, 1968.

Fenton, S., *It All Happened*, Dublin: Gill, 1948.

Fitzmaurice, E.B., & Little, A.G., *Materials for the History of the Franciscan Province of Ireland, AD 1230-1450*, Manchester University Press, 1920.

Flower, R., *The Irish Tradition*, Oxford: Clarendon, 1947.

Ginnell, L., *The Brehon Law*, London: Unwin, 1894.

Gallagher, M.P., *Clashing Symbols*, Darton, Longman, Todd, 1977.

Hanson, W. G., *The Early Monastic Schools of Ireland*, Cambridge: Heffer, 1927.

Hayes, R., *Old Irish Links with France*, Dublin: Gill, 1940.

Healy, J., *The Life and Writings of St Patrick*, Dublin: Gill, 1905.

Henry VIII, *State Papers, Ireland*, 1834.

Hennessy, W. M. (ed.) *The Annals of Loch Cé*, London: Longman, 1871.

Hutton, A. W., (ed.) *Arthur Young's Tour in Ireland*, 2 vols, London: Bell, 1892.

Hyde, D., *Poems from the Irish*, Dublin: Allen Figgis, 1963.

Johnston, F., *Adict for Christ*, Dublin, n.d.

Kavanagh, P., *Collected Poems*, London: Martin Brian & O'Keeffe, 1972.

Kennelly, B., *A Drinking Cup*, Dublin, 1970.

– (ed.) *The Penguin Book of Irish Verse*, Middlesex: Penguin, 1970.

Knott, E., *Irish Classical Poetry*, Cork: Mercier, 1973.

Lecky, W., *A History of Ireland in the 18th Century*, 5 vols, London: Longmans, 1896-8.

Lucius, G., *Cambrensis Eversus*, 3 vols, Dublin, 1848.

MacCana, P., *Celtic Mythology*, New York: Hamlyn, 1973.

MacCarthy, B. (ed.) *Annala Uladh – Annals of Ulster*, 4 vols, Dublin 1887-1901.

MacErlain, *Duanaire Dháibhidh Uí Bhruadair*, (3 vols), *ITS*, London, 1910-17.

McKenna, SJ, (ed) *Dán Dé, The poems of Donnchadh Mór Ó Dálaigh, & the religious poems in the Duanaire of the Yellow Book of Leckan*, Dublin: Educational Company of Ireland, 1922.

– (ed.) *Dánta Aongus Fionn Ó Dalaigh*, Dublin, 1919.

McLysaght, E., *Irish Life in the 17th Century*, Dublin: Talbot, 1939.

McManus, S., *The Story of the Irish Race*, New York: Devin-Adair, 1969.

McNally, R., (ed.) *Old Ireland*, Dublin, 1965.

McNeill, E., *Early Irish Laws and Institutions*, Dublin: Burns, Oates & Washbourne, 1935.

McNeill, M., *The Festival of Lughnasa*, Oxford, 1962.

Macquarrie, J., *Pathways in Spirituality*, Bristol, 1972.

Mac Suibhne, P., *Paul Cullen and His Contemporaries*, 4 vols., Naas: Leinster Leader, 1962.

Meyer, K., *Selections from Ancient Irish Poetry*, London: Constable, 1928.

Madgett, N., *Constitutio Ecclesiastica, 1753-1774*, (MS in Diocesan Archives, Killarney.)

Moriarty, Dr., *Allocutions to the clergy and Pastorals*, Dublin: Gill, 1884.

Mould, D. D. C. Pochin, *Irish Pilgrimage*, Dublin: Gill, 1955.

–*Ireland of the Saints*, London: Batsford, 1953.

Montalembert, Count de, *The Monks of the West*, 7 vols., Boston: Noonan, n.d.

Murphy, G., & Knott, E., *Early Irish Literature*, London 1966.

Murphy, G., *Early Irish Lyrics*, Oxford: Clarendon, 1956.

MacCrócaigh, P., *Prayers of the Gael*, Edinburgh, 1914.

O'Connell, M.R., (ed.) *The Correspondence of Daniel O'Connell*, I.U.P., 1972.

O'Connor, F., (ed.) *A Book of Ireland*, London, 1971.

Ó Corráin, D., et. al., (ed.) *Sages, Saints and Storytellers*, Maynooth: An Sagart, 1989.

Ó Cuív, B., (ed.) *Seven Centuries of Irish Learning*, Cork: Mercier, 1971.

O'Curry, E., *Manners and Customs of the Ancient Irish*, 3 vols., Dublin: Kelly, 1873.

O'Donoghue, D.J., (ed.) *Poems of James Clarence Mangan*, Dublin: Gill, 1903.

O'Dwyer, P., *Céilí Dé, Spiritual Reform in Ireland 750-900*, Dublin: Táilliúra, 1981.

– *Towards a History of Irish Spirituality*, Dublin: Columba, 1995.

Ó Fiaich, T., *Gaelscrínte san Eoraip*, Baile Átha Cliath: FÁS, 1986.

Ó Faoláin, S., *The Irish*, Hammondsworth: Penguin, 1969.

Ó Floinn, D., *The Integral Irish Tradition*, Dublin, n.d.

O'Halloran, S., *History of Ireland*, New York: Virtue, n.d.

O'Hanlon, T., *The Minstrel of Erin*, Dublin, 1930.

Ó Laoghaire, D., *Ár bPaidreacha Dúchais*, Baile Átha Cliath: FÁS, 1975.

– *Our Mass Our Life*, Dublin: Messenger, 1968.

Ó Súilleabháin, S., *A Handbook of Irish Folklore*, Dublin: Educational Company, 1942.

O'Sullivan, D., *Carolan*, 2 vols., London, 1958.

Plummer, C., *Vitae Sanctorum Hiberniae*, 2 vols., Oxford: Clarendon, 1910.

Pope Paul VI, *Evangelization in the Modern World (Evangelii Nuntiandi)*, London: CTS, 1975.

Power, P., *The Book of Irish Curses*, Cork: Mercier, 1974.

Power, P., Canon, *A Bishop of the Penal Times*, Cork: CUP, 1932.

Purcell, M., *The Making of Matt Talbot*, Dublin 1972.

Rolleston, T. W., *A Treasury of Irish Poetry*, London, 1915.

Ryan, J., *Irish Monasticism*, Dublin: Talbot, 1931.

Sigerson, G., *Bards of the Gael and Gall*, Dublin, 1907.

Stokes, W., (ed.) *Féilire Oengusso Céilí Dé – The Martyrology of Oengus the Culdee*, London: Williams, 1905.

– (ed.) *Lives of Saints from the Book of Lismore*, Oxford: Clarendon, 1890.

Stokes, W., & Strachan, J., (eds.) *Thesaurus Palaeohibernicus*, 2 vols., Cambridge, 1901-03.

Waddell, Helen, *Beasts and Saints*, London: Constable, 1934.

Wakeman, W. F., *Three Days on the Shannon*, Dublin: Hodges & Smith, 1852.

Walker, G.S.M. (ed.) *Sancti Columbani Opera*, Dublin, 1957.

Walsh, M., *Knock: The Shrine of the Pilgrim people of God*, Tuam, 1967.

Articles:

Barry, P.C., The Legislation of the Synod of Thurles 1850, in *ITQ* (26), 1959.

Brady, J., Some Aspects of the Irish Church in the Eighteenth Century, in *IER* (70) 1948.

Carney, J., (ed.) The Poems of Blathmac Son of Cú Brettan, in *ITS* (47).

Ní Chinnéide, S., A New View of 18th Century Life in Kerry, *KAJ* (6), 1973.

Crichton, J.D., New and Views, in *The Furrow* (10), 1969.

De Bhál, T., Patterns of Prayer and Devotion, 1750-1850, in *Studies in Pastoral Liturgy* (3), P. Murray, OSB, (ed.), Dublin, 1967.

Gallagher, M.P., Atheism Irish Style, in *The Furrow* (25), 1974.

Hennig, J., Augustine Gibbon de Burgo: A Study in Early Irish Reaction to Luther, in *IER* (69), 1947.

Larkin, E., The Devotional Revolution in Ireland, 1850-1875, in *AHR* (77), 1972.

Meyer, K., entries in *Ériu*, 1904 sq.

Mooney, C., The Irish Church in the Sixteenth Century, in *IER* (99), 1963.

Murphy, G., Scotti Peregrini, in *Studies* (16), 1928.

Ó Floinn, D., The Integral Irish Tradition, in *The Furrow* (5), 1954.

Ó hÁinle, C., Irish Spirituality, in *The Furrow* (27), 1976.

Ó Laoghaire, D., Irish Spirituality, in *The Furrow* (7), 1956.